Praise for My Ailing Champion

From Discovery Reviews (Reedsy), a leading professional review organization

"Loved it! 😍
From penniless to Ph.D., Demetrius battles family, homelessness, and starvation to seek education and the American Dream.

Synopsis

My Ailing Champion details the harsh environment of the Nazi occupation in Greece and the many obstacles the author faced to get an education in the post-WW II years. Family and community leaders opposed education. The author's mother prevented him from reading books. He overcame all obstacles with heroic persistence and some luck and completed his secondary education. To secure free labor, the author's father promised his support for higher education but twice deceived the son. The sisters' dowries were a significant impediment. Ultimately, the family beat up the author and tossed him into the streets hungry, penniless, and jobless, robbing him of his education dream forever. It was for America to throw a lifeline and enable the author to get a college education, even a Ph.D.

Koubourlis defines education as the ability to apply *critical thinking*. He strives to do so with an honest examination of his life and our world and seeks objectivity in promising dialog of opposing viewpoints; he doesn't shy away from delving into some of the fundamental differences between Communism and Capitalism while suggesting a way to settle diverging viewpoints.

The author expresses his deep gratitude for a chance at the American Dream and bemoans the current state of America, his ailing champion. He casts a hopeful note stemming from America's noble character and long-term aspirations, concluding that, far from being perfect, America is nevertheless the best country the world has ever known.

Demetrius Koubourlis was raised on the Grecian sea waterfront in Rion. The constant stream of travelers affected his love of cultures and sparked a desire for education. This was to his father's dismay as attending a school would keep Demetrius for the main part of the day instead of helping out at the family hotel and restaurant. Greek society was also an obstacle due to the cultural norms that put education on the back burner. Demetrius pursues a love of music and school despite societal norms and familial obstacles by attempting to trailblaze a path that keeps him from an existential crisis of mental complacency and raises him out of homelessness.

He does a great job of addressing the indoctrination that results from our cultural upbringing to show how he has come to understand and interpret the behaviors of those around him throughout his life. The novel has many heartbreaking times, but the author always keeps his pride about him. While this is sometimes to his detriment, it allows him to express gratitude for all the chance encounters that have helped shape his life. To break up the story into more digestible chunks, Demetrius offers life lesson chapters reflecting the interplay between moral and societal norms that impact how we view the circumstances that befall us.

Overall *My Ailing Champion* is a great book about betrayal and rising out of a dark situation emphasizing a love for education and the American Dream. ... I recommend this book to readers looking for a challenge as certain parts are high-level reading."

—*Discovery Reviews (Reedsy)*
Reviewed by Amy DiMaio

"From the beginning of the Prologue, I was hooked, couldn't wait to read more, and was not disappointed.

The very personal introspective insights endeared me to this author, who expressed such open honesty in a delightful writing style.

I am grateful for the opportunity to have an in-depth look into this very special person's unique life and adventures. One of the most enjoyable books I have read."

"A very personal shedding of cultural bondage and family conflict . Beginning in a post war Greece. This is a story of a man's innate passion for learning and the restraining circumstances that caused tremendous inner conflict. Not without incredible resilience does he emerge from a long battle to achieve his goals.

This autobiography celebrates the American dream with sincere gratitude from the perspective of an immigrant at a time where his champion struggles to uphold its place in the current global order.

A powerful and deeply courageous baring of the soul makes this a fascinating read from beginning to end.

Unstoppable Demetrius- I hope you have found some peace and happiness."

–Megan Bachmann, South Africa

From Booklife, a leading professional review organization.

"Any dream worth chasing becomes an even more arduous pursuit without social and familial support. This is the premise of Koubourlis's contemplative, plaintive, and ultimately rousing memoir, a story that begins in Nazi-occupied Greece, faces that nation's harrowing three-year civil war, and builds, after agonizing bureaucratic hardship in a system "designed with zero respect for the citizens," to the author's immigration to the United States, where he earned a B.A. and doctorate in just eight years. Doing so involved much sacrifice, including "irrevocable family ostracization" and declining his own inheritance. Koubourlis grapples with family relationships, especially a standoffish mother and an autocratic and abusive father who considered—like many in their community—education "a privilege reserved for the upper crust."

Through sharp, observant writing, Koubourlis recounts an impassioned pursuit of learning in spite of a restrictively traditional culture. Once, his mother burned his newspaper collection clippings, and twice, his father betrays him—denying their deal of financially supporting his study in Italy in exchange for running their grocery store unpaid—by commanding with finality that the dowries of Koubourlis's unmarried sisters come first before his studies. "Ignorance has its own blind strength," Koubourlis notes. "It is intolerant, sure of itself, unreasoning" Still, he persists through ordeals— facing poverty, hunger, and unplanned marriage—but still striving for his dream. There's power in his choice to come to America, a nation he champions: what better way to liberate a thwarted dream than to migrate to a place that claims democracy for all its people?

His striking definition of self-worth— the "protector and motivator in the struggle for success"—powers the narrative, as Koubourlis narrates, with insight and vivid detail, his navigation of indifference, insensitivity, and cultural clash, asking probing questions and sharing sage advice about what it takes to succeed, namely self-worth, wise use of time, and that which happens when preparation meets opportunity—luck. He finds that future in America, and perhaps, through the writing, some peace with the past, too.

Takeaway: Pointed, pained, touching account of coming to America for learning and freedom."

–Booklife

"*My Ailing Champion* is part love letter to America and part epic tale about an extraordinary life. This book would make a great movie, written with insight, peppered with opinions, wit, and Koubourlis' unique perspective. Even though parts of this book are pretty intellectual, I find the writing style to be mostly easy & enjoyable to read.

As a child, the author learned about horror and death firsthand and describes it vividly and with the perspective of his now grown-up, considerable intellect. The wars and the ugly culture created by those wars he describes are disturbing. I think it's essential that we don't forget what a catastrophe war is, and this book helps cement that in the reader's mind.

I found the "Hotel University" section fascinating. A "university," indeed! A curious, intelligent child who loved books couldn't find a more interesting place to learn how to "read" people. Sadly (and unbelievably, to me), his parents did everything they could to prevent him from attending school past the compulsory elementary years. Such a foreign idea to me! My suburban

American parents rewarded me all through school whenever I excelled, and their fervent hope and dream was that I get a university degree. And they were super proud of me when I did. I never imagined that there could be parents out there like Demetrius'.

Returning to the movie theme, he was so determined to learn and loved learning so much for its own sake that I cheered for him as he overcame incredible obstacles to get an education. My heart sang for him when some person crossed his path and helped him in his seemingly sacred educational endeavor. It's easy to get emotionally involved in this story. Your heart can't help but go out to ambitious little Demetrius.

The "love letter" hits high gear with Demetrius' excitement and ambition when he starts his new, grown-up life in America. The cultural differences and life-learning experiences as he works his way through college are sometimes poignant and often humorous, and I enjoyed them a lot. His resilience and persistence in his educational goals are inspirational. Helpful people continue to appear in his life, and he learns from and appreciates every single one. Like (fast) clockwork, he accomplishes his goals. But there is a bit of a cliffhanger ending, suggesting a possible sequel? It is an excellent memoir, surprisingly revealing in some ways and maddeningly mysterious in others. A very interesting, inspiring, motivational read."

– BajaLeslie, USA

"A de profundis baring of one's soul! A dreamer's vicissitudes and the agony of coming of age in Greece. I really enjoyed reading it and identified with most of it. A lot of memorable quotes."

–Chris Poulos, USA/Greece

"In *My Ailing Champion*, Demetrius Koubourlis' memoir, we have a candid self-reflection from the author from an early age. We learn about his hard work and ambitious nature, which allows him to win over adversity and accomplish his goals. This is so despite any parental or family support.

As I read, I found myself cheering him on and wishing him success against all adversity. I continued to read as Koubourlis described honest personal experiences as he wove in historical details. This kept me captivated until the end and left me curious to know more.

I recommend this memoir, *My Ailing Champion*, to anyone who believes in the human spirit, the power of education, personal fulfillment of goals, and in achieving the American dream."

—Dania Schleff, USA/Cuba

"An interesting book about a man who has lived long and seen much. Thought-provoking and highly intellectual."

—Lisa Whitehead, USA

"Praise for an Extraordinary Man and His Remarkable Journey: Demetrius Koubourlis has gifted us with a profound memoir that chronicles the challenges of his boyhood in Greece, painting a vivid portrait of resilience, tenacity, and the indefatigable human spirit. His story is a testament to the power of curiosity, willpower, and intelligence, qualities that propelled him from the hardships of his early life to the shores of the United States.

With an unyielding thirst for knowledge and a relentless drive, he seized every opportunity for education, culminating in a Ph.D. This remarkable achievement is but one chapter in a life characterized by diversity and success, a testament to his extraordinary capabilities and unwavering determination.

His journey reflects a deep curiosity about human nature, an exploration of what motivates people, what shapes a good person, and what leads to failure. His insights offer a profound understanding of what it takes to succeed in life and how humanity can learn from its past to forge a better future.

This book is more than a memoir; it is a beacon of hope and inspiration. It challenges us to reflect on our own lives and encourages us to pursue our dreams with the same vigor and passion. Through his life story, the author has not only chronicled his personal achievements but has also provided a roadmap for others to follow, showcasing the boundless possibilities that lie within each of us."

—Hans Kessel, Switzerland

"This exciting book is a rare and welcome amalgam of books on autobiography and history. While the book centers around Mr.

Koubourlis' life experiences, he doesn't live in a vacuum. The book is deft in critical thinking on why things played out as they did, frequently referencing cultural factors as predominant causes."

–Peter Bo Hansen, Chile/Denmark

(Scroll down for translation).

„Für mich war „My Ailing Champion" eines der Bücher, die mir im Leben am meisten die Augen öffneten. Deshalb war es auch teilweise schwer und traurig, es zu lesen, da wir in viele Abgründe des menschlichen Verhaltens geführt werden, und ich oft nicht glauben wollte und konnte, was ich da las.

Nichts desto Trotz ist „My Ailing Champion" für mich ein positives Buch. Wir dürfen Dank dieser ergreifenden Lebensgeschichte lernen, dass es war ist - die Hoffnung stirbt zuletzt. Egal welche Schwierigkeiten sich uns in den Weg stellen, wenn wir das Ziel klar vor Augen haben kann uns nichts von unserem Erfolg abhalten. Wo ein Wille ist, ist auch ein Weg.

Ich bin zutiefst berührt, dankbar und ergriffen, dass ich auch noch das Glück habe den Autor persönlich zu kennen und viele Worte und Geschichten direkt aus seinem Mund hören darf.

Demetrius Koubourlis ist ein Mann, den es lohnt kennenzulernen, und seine Bücher zu lesen ist sicher das Zweitbeste, das man tun kann. Ich bin der festen Überzeugung, dass jeder aus seinen Worten genau das schöpfen kann, was ihm oder ihr im Moment auf dem eigenen Lebensweg am besten nützt.

„My Ailing Champion" ist ein faszinierendes Buch, das eine faszinierende Lebensgeschichte erzählt. Ich werde es auf jeden Fall immer im Gedächtnis halten, und es als einen der Wegweiser für mein eigenes Leben sehen und nutzen."

(Translation:
"For me, "My Ailing Champion" was one of the most eye-opening books of my life. That is why it was sometimes difficult and sad to read it, as we are led into many abysses of human behavior, and I often didn't want to and couldn't believe what I was reading. Nevertheless, "My Ailing Champion" is an optimistic book for me. Thanks to this poignant life story, we can learn that it is true -- hope dies last. No matter what difficulties stand in our way, if we have

our goal clearly in mind, nothing can stop us from succeeding. Where there is a will, there is a way.

I am deeply touched, grateful, and moved by the fact that I am also lucky enough to know the author personally and to have heard many words and stories directly from his mouth. Demetrius Koubourlis is a man worth getting to know, and reading his books is undoubtedly the second-best thing you can do. I firmly believe that everyone can draw from his words precisely what is best for him or her at a given moment on their own path in life.

"My Ailing Champion" is a fascinating book that tells a fascinating life story. I will always keep it in mind and use it as a guide for my own life.")

–Franziska Norman, Germany

"I really enjoyed reading this account of Demetrius' life and his early struggles. The book is well-written, easy to understand, and keeps the reader engaged in learning about Demetrius' childhood and later in his adult years in the U.S.

It was very eye-opening to see his family's bias against education and how the children were supposed to help the family while putting their own futures on hold. This also seemed to be the general cultural attitude towards education in Greece at the time, which I wasn't aware of. This is very different from the cultural importance that education was given as my parents were growing up in India in the 1950s and 1960s. Back then, education was seen as a crucial means by which families could become upwardly mobile and parents greatly supported their kids' efforts at becoming educated while still helping out the family at home. This is also very true of India today.

Demetrius' writing style gave me a vivid description of the intense struggles he had to face in order to pursue his educational dreams and how much getting an education meant to him. Despite all the obstacles in his way, I cheered him on each step of the way as he started to achieve his goals and ambitions. The various photos of his family through the years was also a nice touch -- it helped to put a face to the various people in his life...

Overall, I really liked the book and Demetrius' writing style. It's very easy to follow, keeps the reader engaged and you want to keep reading to see how it will all turn out."

"I finished reading the book. I found it to be a very good read. The historical facts about Greece were very enlightening. A very well-written life story. I also like the artwork."

From Kirkus Reviews, a leading professional review organization:

"An often absorbing, if occasionally polemic, immigration remembrance and defense of the American dream.

In this memoir, a Greek immigrant to the United States who's also a linguistic scholar shares his version of the American dream.

The book opens in 1994 in a restaurant in the Cook Islands, where Koubourlis listened to an anticolonial anarchist at a nearby table pontificating on the history of American exploitation. As an immigrant who viewed the United States as a "savior," the author stood up to publicly debate the stranger on American virtues. This introductory anecdote sets the tone of the memoir, which centers on how the U.S. opened up educational, professional, and other opportunities for the author. The book's first half centers on his life in his home country of Greece. Born during his own nation's civil war, Koubourlis had a childhood that included homemade bomb shelters and other wartime horrors that he later featured in his short story collection, Sometimes Cruel (2023). The current book mostly focuses on his desire, as a young adult, for an education: "I was locked into a family and community conspiracy," he writes, describing himself as suffocated by the "war-traumatized mediocrity" of his family's psyche. Hungry for education, the author expressed dismay that his mother banned books from their home and encouraged him to find a trade or enlist in the military. To escape the limited opportunities of his motherland, Koubourlis immigrated to America in 1959 to attend California State College in Sacramento; the author recalls his awe at first seeing the Statue of Liberty and skyscrapers as his ship approached New York City. Over the course of the next two decades, his life centered on what he calls an "educational marathon." Koubourlis would earn a doctorate from the University of Washington's Slavic and East

European Languages and Literatures Department and later become a tenured professor.

Although the author notes the highlights of his career, which included the publication of multiple scholarly books and his service as a foreign-exchange professor in the Soviet Union, much of his book is dedicated to his admiration of the nation he now calls home. Never one to back down from a philosophical debate, he notes his public squabbles with Ivy League Marxists, whom he describes as "ideological sleepers on the alert for any opportunity to replay their canned message." Although he's critical of American politicians driven by "crisis-driven policy," Koubourlis emphasizes his belief that his adopted country's "core ideals align with a better world." Those on the left of the political spectrum may disagree with his defense of American exceptionalism, as well as some of his policy positions, such as his argument that immigration authorities should prioritize "the cream of the crop." But the book's narrative offers an inspirational read when it's focused on the author's personal triumphs. The author employs an accessible, engaging style that's distinct from that of his peer-reviewed, academic writings. The text is accompanied by full-color maps, photographs, and other images, although some of the book's AI-generated artwork detracts from the narrative.

An often absorbing, if occasionally polemic, immigration remembrance and defense of the American dream."

–Kirkus Reviews

For updates, click Koubourlisbooks.com.

MY AILING CHAMPION

Demetrius Koubourlis PhD

Axios Eclectics

"An unexamined life is not worth living."
                                   --A distant ancestor.

Table of Contents

Prologue

elf-birth

S "We need to destroy it all, to tear it down and not give a damn about improving. Nothing's worth improving. Keep destroying. Satisfy your needs and desires," the young lady at the head of the table was proclaiming. As I had nothing better to do, I tuned in to the conversation so near me. A family of about a dozen was wrapping up their dinner.

It was in 1994. I was in the South Pacific, dining alone at a small Cook Islands restaurant. A hula dancer had just finished her alluring hip-gyrating number.

This is nihilism, I thought to myself. I had heard it all before.

"All ideologies are defective," she continued, "all societal norms are wrong, and all social structures are meaningless."

This sophomoric depiction was by now getting to me. But there was more to come:

"Get rid of all institutions, political frameworks, and cultural values. Don't waste your time and energy trying to improve America – it's pointless and futile. All existing systems in America must be torn down."

I had heard enough and just could not take it anymore. As if suddenly stung by a scorpion, I jumped to my feet.

"Excuse me!" I said, unable to control the tone of my voice or behavior and not even thinking about what I would say. "How right the young lady is; sure, there were no houses, roads, electricity, or infrastructure before. Why do we need them now? Why do we need airplanes? The young lady swam here all the way from New York City. And she even gave birth to herself, raised herself, planted the crops and harvested the fields, built the roads and trucks, and brought electricity here tonight. Oh, yes, the meal and the drinks we all enjoyed this evening fell from heaven."

I had only gotten started, and it seemed I would never stop. The people around me in the small restaurant initially looked at me as if I was crazy. In rapid succession, their faces began lighting up like light bulbs one after another until they were all lit. Well lit. They began nodding their heads in approval with every point I was making. The young lady seemed at a loss. She had been broadsided. Unexpectedly.

"All you people want to do is destroy, tear down, and offer nothing in its place." I continued, somewhat emboldened. "You depress me. You lack substance and purpose. *What's the matter with you?*"

Then I sat down and shut up.

I had also shut *her* up. I felt relieved no one had attacked me physically. The couple at the table across from me silently clapped when our eyes crossed. The waiter approached my table with a fresh beer – "It's from the gentleman over there by the bar," he said, pointing to a man sitting on a stool raising his drink. I acknowledged the gift by lifting my glass in his direction.

We have some friends here, I thought.

And I indeed needed that beer just there and then. Like a pufferfish, I hastened to pass that cold liquid through my lips to increase my defenses.

The nerve that young person had! America, the country she was deriding, was my savior; its institutions and people had thrown me a lifeline and enabled me to reach enviable heights. I was not about to sit there and *allow* such abuse. I owed it to America to rise in its defense out of mere decency.

Come on, people! Don't we, immigrants, and all children of American immigrants, owe America something?

DEMETRIUS KOUBOURLIS PHD

PREFACE

*E*ducation? No way!
  What if you aspired to higher education, but everyone around you believed it was impossible without money or political clout? What if your own family were against education and prevented you from getting one, exploiting you, beating you, and tossing you into the streets hungry and penniless? Would you then give up?

I was born in Greece.

Greece had just emerged from six years of World War II and was in the grip of a brutal three-year civil war as I was growing up. Dark, perilous, and pessimistic times. Brother killing brother, father and son killing each other -- killers on the loose.

I wanted an education.

The response was loud and clear: Everyone discouraged me from pursuing my education with absolute finality and authority:

"Forget about it!" was the general chorus.

"You've got to help with your sisters' dowries" was my family's mantra.

"You need to do your military service. You owe a duty to your country," was the community president's response.

All doors were shut. The deck was stacked against me. My future had been programmed for me. There was no choice. The mentality was: "We're all in the same situation. We're all together; who are you to flee? No higher education for you! Period."

I was locked into a family and community conspiracy, a captive, a prisoner, and a slave, suffocating by the war-traumatized mediocrity that encircled me like a thorny noose around my neck. That environment was not about education; it was all about survival -- totally existential.

Education was a privilege reserved for the upper crust. It was only for the fortunate few, the rich, and the well-connected. Everyone else, get lost!

Desperate for success
I was an avid reader.

Literature, history, and foreign languages fascinated me. My reading must have engendered the notion that possessed me: I always thought destiny had a loftier design for me. I was unsure of what it was. Still, I dared to hope it would be higher than most, if not all, of my peers in my limited social environment. I imagined myself as a successful and respected individual embarking on a fulfilling journey through life. I knew that education was my only option, a necessity. I craved knowledge and distinction, but a gluey mass of confident and comfortable ignorance held me back; it filled every void around me, poisoning my being with asphyxiating despair.

I had to make a name for myself; I had to succeed!

The bleak future I faced meant spending the rest of my life working for my authoritative and abusive father's small family businesses. That could not possibly have been a viable alternative for me. In my idealistic adolescent mind, death seemed preferable.

Not through perseverance alone
One can endure a great deal for a worthwhile goal.

Persistence and perseverance helped me overcome obstacle after obstacle to burst out of the oppressive abyss of collective obstructionism, earn a high school diploma, and step into the beautiful world of university education. Indeed, as I found myself inundated with incredible educational opportunities in the United States, I am baffled as to why so many people do not value and don't take advantage of them.

Oh, how I regret that I have only one life to live!

Along the way, fortuitous encounters proved pivotal, some in a good way, some not. Showing gratitude is an integral part of man's better nature. However, we forget to do so often. When we show appreciation, we pause to acknowledge someone who has benefited us and reward ourselves for doing the right thing. I am deeply grateful to all those good people whose intentional or unintentional actions benefited me.

One's life is like that. It contains unplanned, unexpected, and surprising pivotal moments, which can be beneficial or harmful. They can lift us up or drag us down. We do not control them or know why or where they come from. Whether they fill us with joy or sorrow, they significantly alter our lives. But we must be alert to perceive their occurrence and respond whenever possible.

Occasionally, in my less rigorous intellectual moods, as I try to comprehend and explain the timely appearance of certain people at singular moments in my life's path, I flatter myself, wondering if some extraneous caring force has not been looking out for me. The skeptic's skeptic that I am, I go no further.

Why this book

Along my life's path, people familiar with some details of my educational marathon have urged me to document it, confident that it would inspire others to dream, persevere, and pursue their academic goals regardless of obstacles.

While acquiring my formal education, my cultural heritage clashed with other cultures; I was forced to scrutinize and reexamine long-established social and religious premises and thereby gain substantial enlightenment. The multicultural and multi-lingual exposure shaped me *beyond formal education*. It provided the equipment to think better; it opened my mind to other possibilities, allowing critical thinking to replace darkness, pushing ignorance aside, avoiding it, fighting it, and keeping it sequestered.

I consider this the culmination of my life's achievements.

This is why I decided to write this book; otherwise, why would anyone be interested in my life's details?

I believe education is one of the most worthwhile goals in life. Education should be a life-long process for everybody according to their aptitude and resources. It does not need to be academic or vocational, but it should be mind-opening. Education helps one become a better human by cultivating the highest of our assets, our minds.

Socrates' *examined life* is all about juxtaposing one's life events with the advantage of hindsight, getting a sharper focus, comprehending, and extracting more sense. When confronting events in isolation, we miss the contrastive aspect -- we do not examine one event in the background of another, one occurrence as a cause or a consequence of another. We are prone to forget and rationalize, to revise and rewrite life's events in some favorable light.

Be careful what you remember.

An "examined life" must also be an *examining life,* a probing life. This is a much broader goal, one of a loftier nature. Granted, an examined life leads to a better understanding of oneself. But it also sharpens the tools for a more enlightened examination of our world, enabling critical thinking.

We are born ignorant. Ignorance breeds intolerance and vulnerability; intolerance necessitates action and elicits strong emotions. It has been said that you should not make assumptions; the most common assumption we make is that we know. We'd be more cautious if we knew that we didn't know. Above all, a good citizen must develop critical thinking skills and an enlightened mindset.

This is what I have aspired to do.

An examined and probing life leads to a cultivated, evolved, and developed life. What a developed life might be is an individual matter. It could include developing latent talents and utilizing more time to create. At all events, it would undoubtedly have to be a life beyond mere "consuming."

I consider the true culmination of a probing life to be an evolving one that is anxious to improve and ameliorate itself and its milieu in all its forms.

∞∞∞∞

As events unavoidably involve others who may be unavailable to present their viewpoint or defend themselves, aspiring to objectivity is imperative.

Objectivity is the path to the truth, but it is also challenging to attain. Our prejudices stemming from social, cultural, or individual perspectives obstruct objectivity. We tend to nurture and develop prejudices of all kinds. Tendencies exist within us; given the right stimulus, they go unbound. How do you feel toward fat people, short people, dark-skinned ones, people with an accent? Check yourself the next time you go to Walmart. How would you classify your neighbors? Why do you like some and not others, and what may change your liking? What do you think of your associates' politics? Did you notice what they subscribe to and how you feel about that? And what about Gatekeeping? Do you believe it's fair to restrict those you disagree with but not those you agree with? What if you were treated that way yourself?

Indeed, biases proliferate. Doubt yourself next time you feel inclined to pat yourself for your exemplary objectivity. Objectivity is not an achievable destination but a beacon showing the right path.

I am keenly aware that autobiographies, by their very nature, are subjective. I have striven to be as objective as possible, considering that such a lofty goal is challenging and occasionally unattainable. To that end, I have relied on my extensive diaries and correspondence rather than my fickle memory as I tried to understand and explain the world from the current status of my consciousness.

I must also admit that I have been selective as well. There's no way to account for all events in one's life. Writing sheds light but also raises questions, and it is an opportunity for further writing. Occasionally, an alert reader would like to know more about an area the author hinted at but failed to develop. It's understandable. By necessity, a writer must choose a path and its supporting material. Thus, selectivity is inevitable.

∞∞∞∞

I used Microsoft's amazing Bing Image Creator and exploited Microsoft Design's technology to generate and alter most of the pictures in this book. Their visual context is purported to be of the times, with ethnicity, clothing, technology, and more taken into account. It's almost like being there and taking pictures at that time. I am grateful for such a dream gift, which, without AI, would have been unthinkable until recently. This is a time-consuming, creative effort that is interactive and gratifying. For example, this book's cover alone took over two months to produce. There was always some detail that didn't correspond to my developing expectations. And then, there was more until it finally felt like a good fit had emerged. I confess I may have gotten carried away with some pictorial flourishes. I hope you will enjoy these AI pictures as much as I did creating them.

I am also indebted to Leslie Sullins for being a tireless sounding board and for her general assistance.

This book is dedicated to all the eager intellects, extant and future, who cannot wait to improve our world.

VOLUME I: GREECE

DEMETRIUS KOUBOURLIS PHD

1. WW II Memories

Killers on the loose

*K*illers on the loose
My first memory from the war appears in my *Sometimes Cruel: Short Stories.* It describes the horror of a two-and-a-half-year-old toddler running behind his mother to a homemade bomb shelter. At the same time, the Italian biplanes above hurry to drop their lethal load during the busiest hour in the center of Patras, seven kilometers away.

The Italian bombs killed and maimed many innocent civilians that day and on subsequent raids. Just imagine: crowds at the center of town, people going about their business as usual, then within minutes, blood flowing in the streets, limbs scattered about, slaughtered bodies all over.

Why?

I wonder what Vivaldi or Verdi would think if they knew their descendants would commit or were capable of such atrocities.

The Greek Holocaust

I can still see in my mind's eye the freight cars parked on the railroad tracks across from our house; they were waiting for the train from the opposite direction to pass – they were packed with disheveled men and women standing close to each other, looking desperate and lost. These people were mainly Jews carted like cattle to death camps; they had been rounded up, most likely from the Peloponnese and the nearby Islands. I surmise they were being gathered in Patras and shipped north to Salonica and from there to the camps in Auschwitz-Birkenau in occupied Poland. I recall, as a five-year-old, loitering near the German soldiers who were standing by the open barb-wired freight car doors with machine guns at the ready. I remember brochures vilifying the Jews strewn about on the main road in front of my father's shops.

Did I understand what was going on at the time? Probably not. I was most likely taking it in as another occurrence of everyday life.

But the most extensive Jewish round-up occurred in Thessaloniki (Salonica), a city in northern Greece that had a population of 160,000 when the Nazis invaded Greece. About one-third of them were Jews. They had been established there for centuries and enjoyed full Greek citizenship. They thrived as a commercial and cultural center, minding their own business and presenting no threat to the German nation. In 1944, the Nazis, wasting no time, rounded up an estimated 60,000 and deported them to concentration and labor camps. They also scooped up Jews from Ioannina and Athens as well as from other parts of Greece.

Almost all of them were murdered.

By what luck of the draw were these people born Jewish, and that a madman would convince a whole *Christian* nation to perpetrate the worst of crimes? I often thought: If my family were Jewish, we would have been on those freight cars.

What's so criminal about being Jewish? What could possibly inspire such atrocities?

I made it a point to visit several of the concentration camps and even took my children to some by way of a solemn pilgrimage to honor and remember the victims.

Some things must never be forgotten.

The Greek massacres

In 1943 when I was five years old, in Kalavryta, a mountainous village in Peloponnese only 25 miles away from my birthplace, German Nazis rounded up all males and gunned them down in a field. At the same time, they forced all the women and children into a school building and set it on fire. A total of about 700 civilians lost their lives that day in retaliation for the killing of 70 German soldiers by the Greek Resistance – ten Greeks for each German. Terror ran through the heart of the land. I was too young to remember conversations. But I remember the dread and overall caginess; people were terrified and tended to mind their business -- a lugubrious atmosphere.

A second massacre took place in Crete's Viannos area. The Wehrmacht forces massacred 500 Cretan civilians in retaliation for their support of the Resistance movement.

∞∞∞∞∞

I made it a point to visit Kalavryta and Viannos during one of my visits to Greece by way of a solemn pilgrimage to honor and remember the victims, the same as with my visit to the Nazi concentration camps. Although one can clearly see the horrendous crime in both instances, identifying the motive is difficult.

To wit, the perpetrator is ethnically the same – the German Nazis. The victims, Jews and Greeks, are not. The Greeks were killed as a reprisal for the killing of German soldiers by the Greek Resistance. In retaliation to what did the Nazis exterminate the Jews for? Leaving the fact that the Germans had no business occupying Greece, the question remains: why did they kill the Jews? The answer must be because they hated them. And the obvious question is why.

Evil must be part of the answer. Evil is what worries me about my fellow humans. In all of human history, people have shown they do not hesitate to kill each other. Without difficulty, they fabricate excuses, and off they go, creating havoc, pain, suffering, and destruction. As a reward, they plunder in the process.

Will we ever learn? Not likely. On the contrary, much ingenuity, effort, and expense are regularly invested in finding more efficient ways to kill, more resourceful means to practice evil.

Containing evil is a significant task for humans as a species and a civilization. In my opinion, critical thinking, eliminating intellectual darkness, casts a small ray of hope. Analytical reasoning is not a panacea and will not eliminate evil, but it should control it somewhat. The more enlightened our world is, the better. However, my prognosis is very pessimistic; with every passing year, our ability to commit evil grows, and our capacity to control it diminishes. It is this consistent march of folly towards self-destruction, towards Armageddon, that leads to the supposition that such may have happened before.

In *Sometimes Cruel: Short Stories (My First Memory)*, I suggested the creation of a Global Superforce "with teeth" as a promising solution.

An ignoble death

I recall the late afternoon train returning from Athens. It stopped at the railroad station across from our house for some passengers to get off. As I was loitering in the front of our store, I saw a middle-aged man slowly walking toward our home. He carried a small bundle over his shoulder; he sat under the eves of the neighbor's house and lay down, resting his head on his bundle. I thought that served a dual purpose: to recline his head and ensure it was not stolen.

I told my mother about the man. She admonished me to stay away from him because there were diseased people around.

The following morning, the man lay there still in the same position. I had gotten up early as I was curious. I went closer and looked at him for a while and noticed he was motionless.

"Pε!" (Eh!) I said. There was no response. I picked up a pebble and gently tossed it toward him. Still no response. Fearing the worst, I ran back into the house.

My mother was busy with morning chores and had not been outside yet. I told her the man was still where he lay the night before. My mother repeated the same warning as the day before but decided to look for herself after a while.

"He's dead." She said matter-of-factly. She then instructed me to run to a neighbor's house to ask for help to take the corpse away. Two of the neighbor's grown boys came carrying a homemade ladder, which they placed on the ground parallel and next to the body. Avoiding hand contact, they "rolled" the body on the ladder with a thick stick.

"He probably died of hunger; his stomach was swollen," said my mother in her life-hardened way.

They whisked the body away, never to be seen again.

This must have been during the German occupation when a famine from 1941 to 1944 killed an estimated 5% of the Greek population (200,000 to 300,000). People were dying literally on the streets.

Scraps for survival

Wars bring hunger. Wars bring famine. Wars bestialize people.

My resourceful father managed to keep us adequately fed throughout those awful years. It was not so with everybody. People generally starved. In those pre-refrigeration days, unsold meat from my father's butcher shop would occasionally spoil – I remember this well. At times, spoiling flesh had to be thrown out to feed hungry dogs. At challenging times, like during the German occupation, I recall seeing people chasing the dogs off to grab the rotting meat that my father threw away.

The ecosystem was affected, too. Many birds would fly around during the occupations -- swallows, ducks, geese, and pigeons. Also, closer to the cape's point, the swamp was full of frogs. But as soon as the occupiers left, all the fowl disappeared. For some reason that I could not understand, even the frogs from the swamp by the cape were gone. Then, the fish became scarcer. It was an open secret that dynamite, although illegal, was used to kill fish with abandon at nighttime.

A much-talked event occurred one night. Our community was buzzing with awe the following morning. Some of the local boys had used dynamite close to a sunken German barge, which was loaded with explosives. The detonations threw one of the locals many meters high above the water, it was said. He fell back into the water and survived.

The ecosystem was not the only victim. I witnessed locals remove bricks and more from the Venetian fortress without paying attention to its historical value. Those walls had survived hundreds of years only to be desecrated by the bestialized population as the war's consequence.

Yeah, wars bring out the worst in all of us. You're kidding yourself if you think you are an exception.

Hotel University

Rion or Rio, my birthplace, is a geographical point of great importance for Greece. It is the narrowest sea passage between the Peloponnese and mainland Greece. I spent the first eighteen years of my life there.

My father created and maintained several small businesses that kept the entire family busy most of the time. Our little hotel and restaurant were fortuitous venues for my personal development. Travelers and truck drivers would spend the night in Rion or Antirrion, on the opposite side of the water narrows, waiting for the ferry to take them across the next day. Our hotel and restaurant were the only convenient establishments in Rion to have supper and rest for the night on those days. Consequently, a continuous stream of travelers, some more interesting than others, passed through daily. And some profoundly affected my education.

My job at the restaurant was to put a glass of water on the table when the customers sat down or to fetch something like cigarettes from the "Periptero," a small street kiosk nearby laden with various small stuff. While hearing all sorts of discussions, I absorbed the changing atmosphere with intense interest and delight. It was like a live movie. I was boundlessly curious, and the material was serendipitous and abundant.

Our small restaurant's patrons, primarily of the working class, would talk amongst themselves and across table boundaries. There was a certain loose camaraderie. They had all been going through socio-political upheavals -- wars, occupations, and endless hardship. They all shared something: they were apprehensive fellow travelers; they had come from somewhere and were going somewhere. And they were now joined for the night under one roof, waiting for the next day's ferry. Each had a story to tell, where they came from and where they were going – typical topics. Occasionally, my alert ear would pick up less mundane discussions. I learned to tune in, absorb any proffered essence, and justify time away from my reading. It was reading of a different kind. Undoubtedly, it was excellent schooling, the type that no school can offer – it was the school of real life.

Greek Civil War (1946-1949)

You come to this world and mind your own business, but unbeknownst to you, somewhere, some elemental force has plans for you; you like to be left alone and live your life in peace, but some psychopath somewhere has designs on your fate. You want to grow, learn, and do some good with your life, but evil people will not let you.

Why won't they leave us alone?

World War II had left Greece in ruins. Germans and Italians had done their bit, abandoning Greece's infrastructure in shreds, its institutions wrecked, and its population demoralized and subsisting.

The left-leaning Greek Resistance (EAM) saw an opportunity vacuum after the war; it rose against the government and the monarchy. The Soviet Union threw its support behind EAM. The United States and its allies took the other side.

Fanatics can always be relied upon to do the bidding of big powers. Killing makes more killing possible; it paves the way for barbarism.

And so it was that an idiotic killing spree followed – Greek killing Greek, brother against brother -- bloodshed and more destruction for the poor Greeks and their devastated country.

Will we ever wise up?

The violence against each other even spilled among the school children. The older students organized after-class bloody fights, pitting my brother and me against another pair of brothers for fun. I was not given a choice, but it was with a bloody nose and scratches that I would frequently reach home. Going from school to my house was like a punitive gauntlet to satisfy the entertainment needs of the older bullies in our class.

Grenade for dinner

Another incident stands out: a fearsome traveler ceremoniously sat at the center table of our restaurant one memorable time. As if it were nothing unusual, he removed a grenade from his bundle and demonstrably set it on the table next to where I had placed his glass of water only moments earlier. I took notice, and everybody else did, too. This was during the Civil War.

Cupping his right hand over the grenade, he asked what was for dinner, and my father approached servilely with his gentlest smile and explained what was available. My father was usually not involved in this process. Still, he must have noticed the grenade and taken control of the situation to ensure everything went well. He even offered the man his special "loukanika," a tasty sausage of his own fabrication. All went well, and the man asked for lodging after his meal. Only moments earlier, my father, in the presence of all, had told another client there was no vacancy at our hotel.

How do we tell this grenade-laden, potentially menacing animal that the hotel was full, which indeed it was? Anticipating trouble, my father explained there was no need to worry; he would figure something out. He asked me to go to one of our neighbors, who had previously indicated his house could absorb occasional overflow from our hotel. I ran to the neighbor's house in the pitch dark of the night and, without mentioning the grenade, secured lodging for the guest. We were in luck. That was the end of that episode.

Ike and the Raffle

Some people believe Russia is the West's worst enemy. It does not take a lot of objectivity to derive such a conclusion from history. If America's Manifest Destiny – territorial gain -- was an operative philosophy once, Russia's has always been. It has never ceased to foment turmoil, invade, and try to stay put as if its destiny is to expand its borders forever. And so it was during the Greek Civil War. The Soviet Union wasted no time. As soon as WWII ended with Germany's surrender, the Soviet Union pushed in several directions, grabbing as much territory as possible. This happened at a time when the U.S. was the only country with an atomic bomb. Can you imagine what would have occurred if the Soviet Union had been the sole possessor of the ultimate weapon?

As was mentioned earlier, the Soviet Union was on the side of the Greek communists during the Greek Civil War (1946-1949). The United States' response was the Marshall Plan. The Soviet influence had to be stopped. Rebuilding the economy and the infrastructure was the way. Along with billions of dollars in reconstruction aid, the United States engaged in an information campaign. One occurrence stands out in my memory:

On the other side of the tracks across from our house was the community's central square, the outdoors of the main café, the Kafeneio. This was where men would spend much time drinking coffee, ouzo, or wine, playing cards, smoking, and solving the world's problems. No women ever frequented this man's sanctum sanctorum.

By word of mouth and placards, it was announced that a newsreel would be shown at the Kafeneio for free. All were invited. I decided to go as I had never seen a film and was as curious as possible. I was about nine years old.

Car battery power was used to run the bulky reel-to-reel player. Most oil lamps on tables were turned down to improve the visibility of the black-and-white show.

It was about the U.S., primarily about "Ike," Dwight Eisenhower, whose WWII performance had made him a hero and president. I was fascinated with the glorified presentation. If I had a favorable opinion of the U.S. up to that point, my child's impressionable mind fell in love with Ike and the United States.

You can undoubtedly label this a propaganda effort by the United States. I choose to accept it as an informational service. The other side was also doing its best to (mis)inform. I recall seeing photos of people's throats getting cut with can lids. The Germans had done likewise, dropping leaflets with cartoons defaming the Jews. Let us agree that when your side spreads information, it informs; when the other side does the same thing, it misinforms.

Now that we have that civilized understanding, let us return to the Ike reel and my fascination with the U.S., my grandfather's erstwhile country.

After the show, a big fish raffle was scheduled to entice people to come. Cheap raffle tickets were sold to increase participation. The name of each ticket purchaser was written on a small piece of paper and dropped into a large empty tin oil can. With all the tickets in the can, someone in charge stirred the tickets with his hand and then looked around for someone to pick one ticket.

You can assume there was a small crowd surrounding the oil can. And you can bet that little Demetrius would be at the front within touching distance of the can. People were polite enough to let a nine-year-old creep to the front.

The raffle overseer looked around for someone to draw the winning ticket. He spotted me with my hand raised high. He must have thought a child would be the best choice. So, he asked me to pull a ticket. And I did.

The name on the ticket was my father's!

My father's family. I'm at far right.

Crippling attack

Evil lurks everywhere, it would seem. In times of civil wars, it is like hungry ants lurking in society's cracks for the smell of decaying flesh to come out. The news buzzing through our community after the raffle extravaganza was that the Kafeneio owner had been dragged out of bed at night, beaten unconscious, and abandoned on the main road about a mile away from our home.

His arms and legs were broken, and his head was swollen and barely recognizable. The communists, it was said, did not like that he had allowed the American propaganda, the Ike reel, to be broadcast from his Kafeneio.

Months later, one could see the man sitting in the shade of his café occupying three chairs with crutches by his side. His face was a collage of scars. I never saw the man walk again.

The message was clear:

"Let that be a lesson and warning to all who disagree with us, the sole bearers of the truth. Indeed, if you're not with us, you must be against us, and you deserve to die."

We see this mentality time and again. Dark minds are everywhere; they grow like weeds. The crafty revolutionary or demagogue who dreams of himself controlling society understands this mentality and knows how to exploit it. We have never had a time without some conflict somewhere in human history because we have always had such power-hungry minds and an abundance of gullible, dark minds. A march of folly, indeed.

Education is a credible defense; it can edify minds, enable critical understanding of information, and create enlightened citizens. This is far from easy and may seem too idealistic, but it should not discourage one from trying. Giving up is not an option because evil is an omnipresent force.

Blood aplenty

Another hair-raising memory has left an unsolved mystery for me. One early morning, my brother and I took the 4 to 5 animals my father intended for his butcher shop to a grassy spot in the vast Venetian castle grounds. Using a small staircase exit on the north side across from the seashore, we came up to a massive pile of blood-stained clothing with bullet holes galore. The clothing was not civilian; we could not tell whether it was military or police. We were frightened. We reported it to our parents, who admonished us to keep quiet. A day or two later, someone set the pile on fire.

To this day, I have not found out where those clothes came from. During the civil war, clashes between warring political parties were not infrequent. Infrastructure was a favorite target of anti-government forces that wanted to weaken the government. It was a guerilla war atmosphere with attacks and counter-attacks being the operative mode. Someone always believes that prevailing at all costs is the only way. The hand that offers you a welcome greeting today may pull a trigger to kill you another day. People's tribalism has no cure. It is a disease with many faces.

Firing squad

Another incident involving my father during the Civil War has been described in *Sometimes Cruel*. Blood-thirsty "αντάρτες" (antigovernment insurgents), five or six of them, once came in the thick of the night knocking on our door. They wanted to "talk" to my father. They claimed my father was an agent of their enemy, carrying messages back and forth through the Rion-Antirrion channel. My father did cross the channel to procure animals for his butcher shop, but he was not a messenger of any kind. Unable to convince the trigger-happy people, my father was taken to be shot. Luck, however, was on his side. The leader of the impromptu firing squad was an acquaintance of my father's who vouched for him. They let my father go.

Such a thin line between life and death!

The second time they came for my father was again in the middle of the night. My mother got all four of us kids around my father, perhaps to elicit empathy, pity, or both. My father pulled his shirt open and showed the bandages from his recent ulcer operation, convincing the eager killers that he could not have been where they were accusing him of having been since he was at the hospital.

They never came back.

Marshall Plan

The Marshall Plan, proposed by U.S. Secretary of State George C. Marshall in 1947, was the U.S.'s post-war way to counter the spread of communism and curtail the influence of the Soviet Union. It was established in 1948 when Greece was in the middle of a terrible civil war (1946-1949). The Plan brought needed capital to countries devastated by the Second World War. Infrastructure, factories, and businesses required an infusion of money to be rebuilt.

I was nine years old then. I recall strange-looking dump trucks - - their triangular beds stood out -- noisily passing up and down in front of our house. They were carrying sand to build roads. Our beautiful beaches were defaced, but no one seemed to care then. Ecology was not a priority.

At times, there was a lot of activity in front of our restaurant. People eating, milling around, chatting. I distinctly remember two men conversing with intent. One had a clipboard and was taking notes. The other was speaking in a language I could not understand. I looked at the writing and could understand the numbers. And the words. They were in Greek. This man had been translating his instructions. I had no idea what the foreign language was, but when I brought some water to their table, I asked.

"English, he's an American," said the Greek person, pointing at the foreigner with a slight movement of his head while raising his eyebrows. The American smiled at me in a friendly way. Excellent first impression. I had never seen an American before. I had never heard English before, and I learned that Americans did not speak American but English.

In our family, America was always in our minds; my grandfather and two of his brothers had lived in America for a long time; they helped build the California railroads in the early 1900s. A large hand-knit picture of the American and Greek flags was the sole decoration of our home living room.

Now, a live American was before me. He was sitting at our restaurant, drinking water and eating food, the same as us.

An intense desire took hold of me. I wanted to learn the man's language. I felt envious of the Greek fellow who knew that language. This may have been one of the experiences that awoke a strong interest in foreign languages in me.

UNRRA

One day, our elementary school teacher (there was only one for all six classes.) entered the classroom beaming. With her came a middle-aged man, followed by a younger woman.

"We're fortunate today to have some special guests with us." our teacher announced and introduced the guests. "They have brought you a special present," our teacher continued.

We, war-starved little kids, tried to fit the words with facts to make sense. We were waiting to see the "special present," but the teacher seemed bent on prolonging our agony. She introduced our guests, stating their names and where they came from. All smiles and civility.

That was not a present.

"Where's our present?"

The teacher then solemnly went to the classroom door and opened it. We saw a wheelbarrow cross the threshold and a young man pushing it. The wheelbarrow was loaded with shoe-box-like packages with the UNRRA inscription on the cover. UNRRA stood for the United Nations Relief and Rehabilitation Administration. It was the first United Nations Organization formed in 1943 by Franklin Roosevelt. Its purpose was to provide relief to refugees of World War II.

SOMEBODY CARES

Upon being given a hand signal, the young man placed a single box on our study desks, one before each student.

One cannot imagine the unforgettable excitement.

"This package is yours; it's a present from the United States of America. Enjoy!" the teacher resumed.

I could not wait to open it and find out what was inside. The teacher and our guests left the room, and we were allowed to rifle through our unexpected treasure.

A pencil, a writing pad, some dry biscuits, chocolate, a small bag of marbles, and a rectangular object. What was that? I wondered. I unwrapped the carefully folded corners of the unusual paper to reveal a yellow piece of something. Somebody yelled, "Yellow cheese!" All the kinds of cheese I was familiar with were white. I smelled the thing and was intrigued.

"Yes, cheese!" I heard someone from the other side of the classroom exclaim. I tasted a tiny part of it and, oh, was it ever delicious! And how great it smelled. Before I could gobble it all up, a voice told me to save some for my family. Which I did.

This was my best cheddar cheese experience ever!

DEMETRIUS KOUBOURLIS PHD

2. Education Twilight

*H*igh school? No way!
My god-fearing parents did not value education. The people around me were not educated. What mattered above all was putting food on the table.

Elementary education was obligatory. Schools opened as soon as war conditions permitted. I was lumped into the same class with students of varying ages, most much older than myself. My brother was a year and a half older than me, but some classmates were even five years my senior. Six years later, we graduated from elementary school in the late spring of 1950. This was the first post-World War II elementary school class to graduate -- six years of unimpeded elementary education, a feat, considering the obstacles! I was 12 years old and anxiously ambitious about my future.

OK. Elementary school completed. What next?

One of the community's two "educated" pillars proudly broadcast his decision for his twin boys, our classmates, to continue to high school. Their much older brother, a high school graduate, had been preparing them for the high school entrance exam for a long time.

I had wanted to get help for my brother and me with the exam preparation, but in vain. Father did not really feel it was good to give up two workers. However, he announced that a couple of lessons with the community secretary's older son could get us into high school. I told him we should have prepared long ago, especially algebra. I emphasized we were not ready and would fail. I suppose he was trying to get us in on the cheap like a wise businessman or was setting us up for failure. Or, perhaps, he did not know.

"Never mind. You give it a try." was my father's decision.

You guessed it. My brother and I failed just as I expected. This meant we would have to wait another year before retaking the exam. Father felt satisfied -- he tried to send us to high school like the best of parents, he would claim, but we did not make the cut. It was not his fault.

"Besides, it's really no problem," he assured us, "we have a lot of work here with the family businesses. Your family needs you."

My brother seemed to go with the flow, resigned to his fate -- after all, only two people in the community had finished high school.

But I could not accept life without an education.

Can you possibly feel what it means for an ambitious 12-year-old, enamored with books and learning, to be barred from getting an education? Dejected, disconsolate, and ashamed for failing the high school exam, I went through the daily chores feeling utterly miserable. I was not used to failing. It felt like life was not worth living. *I am never going to amount to anything*, I kept thinking. All my grandiose dreams were going down the drain. I thirsted to change my life, to leave this hopeless environment, but how much could a 12-year-old do?

I dreamt of flying but was forced to crawl.

The Force

Among the guests in our little hotel was a newlywed couple; the man's name was Spiros Psaros, a somewhat older bridegroom with a much younger bride. They lived in Patras, about 7 kilometers away, but decided to celebrate their honeymoon at our little hotel in the suburbs.

The bride spent most of her time in her room. Still, her husband occasionally visited our restaurant, which was located below the hotel. He noticed I filled idle moments with drawings and paintings. He showed intense interest. He was impressed with my work and also saw my brother's work, who could also draw well. He got interested in us and began to ask questions. I wasted no time in sharing our plight with him. He told us he taught "Technics" at the Emboriki Sxoli Patron (Patras Commercial School). Technics had to do with art and commerce.

"There's no reason to despair," he assured me. "Why not come to Emporiki, the commercial school? It's like high school but better because you learn foreign languages, accounting, and more. Moreover, the entrance exam is in the fall, so you will not lose any time; you will be in classes for the fall semester."

It was the first time I heard about Emporiki. I responded that it sounded like a dream, but our father would not let us attend; he needed us there.

"Do *you* want to go?" the teacher asked.

Throw a drowning man anything to stay afloat; you can bet he will take it.

"I'll talk to your father," he promised.

I didn't know what Psaros was telling my father. They seemed to be having more than one discussion over several days. One day, I heard Psaros explain the value of a *commercial* education to my father.

"It's not like high school. Emboriki prepares you for commerce, for business. A commercial education is better."

This seemed to be the key; my father appeared to be listening with more interest. He began to understand that one can make more money with such specialized knowledge. This point was not lost on him. Then, a few days later, he presented "his idea" to us out of the blue.

"OK, I'll let you prepare for the fall Emporiki exam, but you've got to do it without tutors. We have no money for tutors. And you must work harder at our businesses this summer."

I could not believe my ears. I did not quite understand it, but it was a breakthrough. It was totally unexpected and in the nick of time. My gloom was lifted. It felt like a miracle.

I set to work for our upcoming Emporiki exam without wasting time. I can still see my brother and me playfully balancing our bodies on the railroad tracks over a small river near our home while attending to Father's grazing animals. I worked on my brother's doubts and apprehensions and outlined a plan for the daily study of mathematics, which was our Achilles' heel.

My brother and I passed the Emporiki exam and entered our new routine of attending school together.

Oh, God! Thank you, thank you!

When all was lost, good man Psaros had materialized with a solution. What Force placed this man in my path precisely at the needed moment? Lucky coincidence, some will say, and leave it at that.

Really?

To chalk it up to happenstance sounds like a vacuous explanation and fails to answer the question honestly. It merely avoids it. On the other hand, to claim it was some mysterious force out of the universe and the like is a leap I am not prepared to accept either. But simply stating, "I don't know," is what I will offer as the only honest answer as it reflects my belief and accounts for things I cannot comprehend or believe to be beyond our human domain.

No more high school!

It was 1952. I was 14 years old. By this time, my brother and I had attended the Commercial School of Patras for two years. We were good students, especially in Spiros Psaros's Technics class. He loved our artwork and praised us highly. I recall one time, as he was doing his peripatetic explanation in class about some artistic detail, he ruminated out loud:

"If I could afford it, I'd send the Koubourlis brothers to the Athens Art Academy."

My father, the epitome of naked pragmatism, was not impressed when we reported the comments to him.

"Show me how much food that kind of thing can put on the table!" he would frequently say.

So, one day during dinner, he announced to the whole family that my brother and I would *not* continue with school. Henceforth, we were to help him full-time with his businesses. He explained that two years of high school education was enough. We did not need any more schooling, in his estimation. I felt more distraught than ever. I tried to persuade my father to change his decision.

No, it was final.

I tried to recruit my mother's support without success. My brother did not care either way. The whole family aligned with the father – I was all alone then. They began to see me as an outsider -- who do you think you are, Mister? You're one of us, and don't forget it; Father has made up his mind; no appeal is allowed -- that was the attitude.

The Force again

The end of the second semester of the second Commercial School year was approaching. I returned home from school one day after buying cheese from the famed Kefalonia cheese vendors of Patras. My father liked to capitalize on the bus fare to Patras, so after school, I had to occasionally purchase products for our suburban grocery store. A head of cheese, the size of a small car tire, was what I was lugging that day.

Mr. Pitas, perhaps my father's most habitual debtor, happened to be standing beside me on the local bus on the way home to Rion. He was one of those types who treaded on the limits of the law and always seemed to get away. He was shrewd and cunning. And very successful. He was not a poor man. He understood human nature well. Somehow, he managed to get my father to extend credit to him repeatedly before paying for his old debts. He could sweet-talk my father with promises about paying old debts or making small partial payments before getting further credit. And it was mostly about meat. I now surmise he must have come around on Mondays or Tuesdays when people did not buy meat, and unsold meat would spoil in our pre-refrigeration world.

Pitas was a delinquent client; my father had sicked me on him sometime before. Dunning someone like Pitas was a daunting task and the kind I disliked doing. But Father's orders meant losing some adolescent innocence in a hurry.

While the brief bus trip was underway, we made small talk. Pitas asked me about my school, and I shared my sorrow. I told him this would be my last semester ever and that I would not be able to finish high school because my father could not wait four more years to gain full-time services out of me. He would not support my brother and me any further. And his decision was final.

I perceived Pitas' face undergoing visible changes. It was as if he had gotten an under-the-skin massage gadget. His eyes shut and opened again as he looked at the bus floor and into the distance while we held onto the bus support bar. While I observed his changing expressions with interest, he took a breath and uttered an incredible phrase:

"I will support you myself!"

Of course, I could not believe what I heard. This could not be. This man had to be joking. *He must have something up his sleeve*, I thought to myself, as I knew of his reputation. Before my confusion and disbelief settled, the bus stopped in front of my father's store. It was time for me to step off. I thanked him and got off the bus in a daze. *Do you suppose he means it? And how will that work out? And what might he want in return?*

Upon entering our grocery store, I saw my father standing behind the counter.

"Got the cheese? Good. What did you pay for it?" he asked business-like.

I set the heavy head of cheese on the floor, wondering if I should tell my father of Pitas' offer. It was almost 4 p.m., and I had not eaten anything since breakfast, what with the school day and the shopping. I sat down to whatever I could find in the kitchen, some bean soup and bread.

That night, with the family sitting around the table for dinner, I found what I thought was an appropriate moment to mention Pitas' bombshell. I saw my father's eyes roll. He, too, was taken by surprise. He asked me to repeat my account again to ensure he understood correctly. I obliged. We all ate in silence. It was clear something significant was wafting over the dinner table.

"Why did you tell him about your high school plans?" my father asked after a while.

"You know why," I replied most calmly. "My education is the most important thing for me. It is on my mind constantly. I cannot live without it."

Then Father started with his usual ranting spell about the worthlessness of education and how I should stay with him because we would "tie up Patras" with our successful business deals. I let him talk himself out, as my position was more than apparent. I went to bed hoping with all my heart that Pitas' offer was sincere and wondered about my next step.

∞∞∞∞

Saturday was the busiest day of the week for my father's butcher shop. Customers who could afford meat could count on finding freshly butchered meat hanging out al fresco, in the open air. One of my hated assignments was to stand and keep the flies off the hanging flesh with a swatter.

Often, there was more meat available than there were buyers. So, my father frequently ended up with more than he could sell. As there were no refrigerators then, ice was needed to prolong the shelf life of the unsold meat. An ice peddler would bring his horse-driven cart loaded with ice every morning -- block ice was the only way to keep things longer.

On Sundays, the whole family worked hard to prepare for the customers who would stop by for Father's souvlaki or "arni psito" (roasted lamb) with some wine or ouzo. Very often, my job was to keep turning the long metal skewer – another task I hated because of its unfathomably boring potential and the smoke hitting my eyes. The smell did not bother me.

One Sunday, after all the parading community folks concluded their Sunday stroll on the road in front of our shops, we sat down to dinner. It was soon after my conversation on the bus with Mr. Pitas. As it happened, we had a guest that night, a seemingly well-to-do fellow from Athens. He came to spend a few days at our little hotel occasionally. He had led us to believe he was "educated." Indeed, he had even claimed to have traveled around Europe – a detail of immense fascination for me.

Chatting over dinner drifted to us kids and our future. Before I could spill my guts about my school, my father, speaking of me, announced:

"He's continuing with high school; I will make a Venizelos out of him."

I could not believe my ears. I looked at my father, and then, one by one, I took in the expressions of the other family members but said nothing.

I feared Father may have drunk too much wine or been trying to impress our "educated" guest. Venizelos was my father's favorite Greek Prime Minister, Greece's ethnarch, active during the first half of the 20th century. Now, how my father would make a Venizelos out of me is to ponder. As for me, I had difficulty falling asleep that night. Big plans for my future were churning in my head. Something good was afoot.

∞∞∞∞

No one was higher in my father's estimation than the great Venizelos. He was part of my father's limited academic capital. Associating one of his children with the great ethnarch must have been akin to an act of patriotism. And it worked to my benefit. The idea possessed him enough to have assumed super status in his personal dossier. I imagine he bragged about it to whoever would listen as the occasion arose.

I recall one time my father and some diners were discussing national politics. I happened to be standing next to them, ready to serve. Unable to contain myself, I butted in and, walking back and forth like a knowledge-burdened peripatetic professor, expounded on national and international politics. My father turned his chair toward me, stretched his legs, leveled his head, and directed his glance toward me; then, he lowered it and raised it again. He then glanced at the diners and back at me again. He wanted to say something but remained speechless. I had never seen him like that. As was my wont, my discourse notwithstanding, I quickly read his facial display.

The man was gushing with pride.

The association with Venizelos proved of lasting value because my father allowed me to finish high school!

∞∞∞∞

Thus, one chance encounter with Pitas on the bus and his offer to help me with high school triggered a series of consequences to my benefit. Social shame would have engulfed my father had he allowed Pitas to help me through high school; this would have been an unbearable blow to his pride – What? You can't or won't support your deserving son through secondary education, but you would allow a stranger to do it in your place? Pitas' reputation in the community would have risen, and my father's would have nose-dived. My father was coerced into the inevitable decision: he had to permit me to finish high school.

Did Pitas know what he was unleashing? Was his offer an act of altruism? Did he really care for me personally to make that commitment, and would he have carried it out? I doubt any such lofty reasons were in play; it is more likely he was motivated by a strong desire to humiliate my father, whom he viewed as a competitor in our prying community.

Understanding people's emotional "handles" goes a long way to getting them to do what one wants. I wonder what motivates people sometimes to act. Did I know what I was doing sharing my grief with Pitas? Probably not. Did I intend to share my disappointment, despair, and even anger at my father's refusal to help me continue my secondary education? Absolutely, yes.

Four years passed, and I stayed the course until I graduated from high school. I helped around Father's businesses as much as possible, especially in the summers.

OK. High school completed. What next?

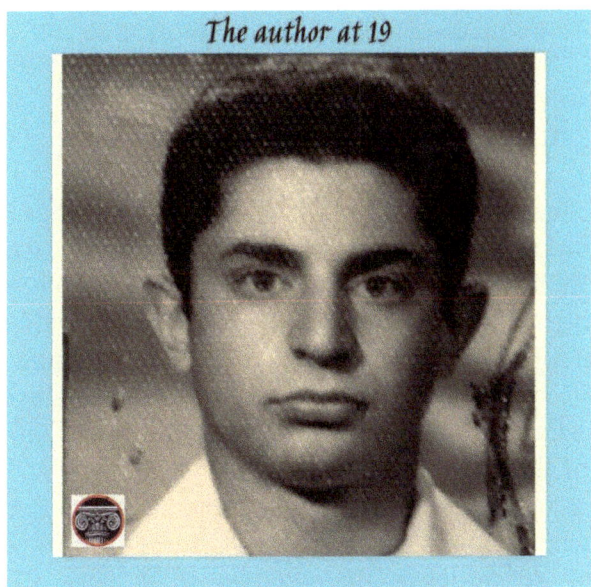

The author at 19

Unworthy of a glorious past

It was common knowledge that applying to Greece's then-two universities of Athens or Salonica was pointless because political clout was required. I never questioned that. It was the standard, indisputable knowledge in our milieu. Even as I write this, I have no idea to what extent, if any, it was correct. There were a lot of misconceptions deeply ingrained in the ordinary mind. What could a teenager do without a reliable information source, like a knowledgeable person, a library, or the Internet?

When I approached the "educated" community leaders about studying abroad, I was given a dismal response.

"The military won't let you. You need to serve," I was informed most authoritatively.

It was like being under a death sentence. There was so much resignation around me; it was the accepted norm; how could one escape it? It felt like being in a slowly sinking ship going nowhere but the bottom. My whole being was boiling with thwarted dynamism; I was pounding my head against an iron ceiling and was suffocating in the shared tank. I had to get out.

I never ceased to believe I would find a way.

The community's secretary and his friend, the community's President, both high school graduates, ranked as the epitome of learned models. As the French proverb says, "In the kingdom of the blind, the one-eyed are kings. (Au royaume des aveugles les borgnes sont rois.)" Our entire community, including my father, respected these two characters but perhaps should not have, as their thinking blocked the path to progress, and they were in my way. Were they guarding their high school supremacy amongst the ignorant?

Only through books and imagination could I find better models.

Lamentably, during the civil war (1946-1949), many intellectuals were targeted by both sides for prosecution and even execution, sometimes by death squads. My ancient Greek forefathers would be ashamed of the state of education in Greece after WWII. Based on my personal experience, the land that gave unsurpassed intellectual gifts to the world was, at this time, steeped in darkness. Socrates, Plato, and Aristotle might wonder if it was all for naught; Archimedes, Euclid, Hippocrates, and Pythagoras would lament inconsolably in the afterworld. From Homer to Herodotus and Aristophanes and up to Kazantzakis, eight thousand-odd years had elapsed, a very long time, and a lot had come to pass.

Creating a high civilization takes many generations, one small step forward followed by another, whether or not in temporal succession. However, destroying a culture does not take long in historical terms. Mankind is more efficient at tearing down than at building up. Centuries of the Roman and Ottoman occupations and their preferred religious belief systems left their mark in Greece, displacing and replacing a glorious past -- one layer instead of another, one layer upon another. The result was intellectual subsistence, not worthy of human potential, and a disappointment compared with ancient Greece's magnificent past.

DEMETRIUS KOUBOURLIS PHD

3. Extracurriculars

*B*urn them!

My parents, especially my mother, discouraged me from reading books. We did not have any books in our house during my early years, except for some medieval lay pamphlets about Mary the Virgin's visit to hell, which my mother regarded as sacred. My mother had a genuine concern about her place after death. She wanted to be in Mary the Virgin's good graces since the holy lady was perceived as the great intercessor, always ready to help sinners through the gate of Paradise. Faith-driven, she insisted I memorize and recite the "sacred" documents every night before bedtime. I opine this exercise had a positive secondary effect – cultivating my memory. I can be grateful for that.

My older sister's romance magazine subscription did not interest me.

My father subscribed to *Peloponnisos*, a local newspaper still in circulation today. I remember him reading it dutifully after his afternoon siesta while enjoying his kafedaki, his Greek coffee demitasse. The historical section on the newspaper's second page piqued my interest; it gave details of the life of Ali Pasha, the ruler of many of the Ottoman Empire's European territories and none other than the one mentioned in *The Count of Montecristo* by Alexandre Dumas (père). I can still see in my mind's eye the cut-out clippings I fondly collected in a shoebox. At first, my mother did not know how to react; after all, the material came from the newspaper my father read regularly. It had to be approved material; it had to be OK. Or was it? She let it simmer for a while but must have wondered about it.

What my parents lacked in education was more than made up for in terms of smarts. They were both of above-average intelligence, especially my father, and could thrive in a harsh environment. One could not tell that my father was not educated. He had mastered standard speech and was arithmetically exceptionally astute. However, complicated Greek orthography was far too inaccessible for him as it is for most Greeks who lack higher education or a better mind.

Mother was the self-appointed authority on what I was permitted to read and what was verboten. After all, she had completed all six elementary education grades, much more than my father's two grades.

One evening, one of the diners at our restaurant impressed my mother as "educated" and worthy of consultation. Aha! This was the chance she was looking for. An "independent" authority had finally landed on her lap. She must have been looking for just such an opportunity. Without wasting time or asking my permission, she brought out my shoebox with the Ali Pasha newspaper clippings. It did not bode well because she held it casually under her arm while serving the man his meal. For some inscrutable reason, I considered that an invasive sign of disrespect for my precious historical collection. She sought the diner's advice, presumably holding her breath.

"Burn them!" the man uttered without the slightest hesitation. And raising his voice, he continued almost reproachfully, "Don't you know who Ali Pasha was?"

My poor mother, a usually sure-footed person, was thrown into confusion. She must have no doubt heard of Ali Pasha, as almost every Greek had. But before she could collect her wits with an answer, the "educated" diner delivered his coup de grace:

"He was a Turk who killed many Greeks." It was uttered with patriotic fervor and accompanied by an emphatic thrust of a small cluster of his partially chewed dinner. It was as if he wanted to be heard by everyone in the restaurant and be admired for the correctness of his view. The man had manifested the well-cultivated national prejudice of hating and fearing the Turks. He was also signaling the narrowness of his intellectual horizon.

"Burn them," he repeated.

That was the last time I saw my newspaper clippings collection. This was an act of intolerance and uncompromising censorship, I felt. It was an oppressive experience not infrequently encountered in an uneducated milieu. History offers several salient examples, from pre-Christian book burning by a Chinese emperor to Christians' burning of the famous Library of Alexandria to Nazis' Kristallnacht, to modern-day Ayatola's fatwas, all leading to the loss of works of cultural and intellectual heritage.

A world map I had attached to the wall soon disappeared as well.

Ignorance has its own blind strength. It is intolerant, sure of itself, unreasoning, and, most lamentably, it can easily be manipulated for severe harm. Isn't ignorance dangerous?

We need enlightenment.

We need enlightenment.
We need enlightenment.

Let me read!

Reading outside the classroom was not encouraged. We had our paltry textbooks, of course. Our Commercial School had no library and no books to check out. There were no books at our house either. Fancy that! Aristotle's descendants had stopped reading! Was it the 400-500-year Turkish occupation that extinguished the reading lights? Was it the wars? Just what was it that doused the Greeks' curiosity for knowledge those days?

Curiosity does not come to dinner unless there is something to eat.

Fortunately, I somehow found out about a small public library in Patras. Asking around, I learned that any teacher could vouch for a student to borrow books. I approached my Gymnastics teacher and gained access to this library with his note.

I remember it well -- a small, single room with a high ceiling. The shelves reached high. On my first time in the library, I was stunned. I had never seen so many books in the same place. Yet, it was a one-room set-up. My glance traveled from one side to the other in awe, wonderment, and excited delight.

I have no idea what the city's library system was at other times. And I had no knowledge of any other library in Patras. I knew there were libraries in monasteries.

I showed the librarian, an older lady of indeterminate age, my teacher's voucher; she took it and wrote my name and particulars on a large register. I was now a member and had access to all those books!

"What would you like to check out?" the librarian asked. I looked at the rows of shelves with more books than I had ever seen and realized I had no particular book in mind whatsoever. All I knew was I needed to read. Anything would do. Quick thinking came to the rescue.

"Let's start at the top left shelf," I said nonchalantly. The librarian looked at me, then another look at her register, and asked:

"Is there any particular author that interests you?"

"Oh, I like most of them," I said because I didn't have a better answer. "But I'd like to start from the top left shelf, please. I am planning to read all of the books here." The lady looked at me once again, adjusting her thick glasses.

"OK. The first book on the top shelf from the left, you say." She got up, pulled a free-standing wheeled ladder, and fished the book out for me. She called out the title and author and asked if that was the book I wanted. I had never heard of the book or its author, but I faked otherwise. She instructed me to return it in two weeks or sooner; otherwise, I would lose my book-borrowing privileges.

"Can I borrow more than one book?" I timidly asked.

"Only one at a time," was the dry answer.

With my book treasure in hand, I ran back to school. Because we lived in Rion, a Patras suburb, it was convenient for me to go to the library while at school. We had a 30-minute mid-morning break. The class break was my chance to run, get the book, and return by the time the classes resumed. Unfortunately, the city library was located a considerable distance from my school. It did not hurt that I was a good sprinter.

With time, the librarian let me check out two books at once. I was able to read many books that way; I learned about the various authors and became discriminating in my reading. My vocabulary shot up. My Greek Composition teacher noticed it. So did my Gymnastics teacher, but he felt insecure whenever I showed off my knowledge.

Some time afterward, a small library debuted in the Patras American Information Service offices. And it was closer to my school. I began borrowing books – some American authors in English and some in translation. I read all of Eugene O'Neil's works or what was available. I discovered Pearl Buck and a few others. The staff soon knew me and would have the new books ready. I read and read, and my thirst for knowledge, like a well-watered plant in the sun, increased by leaps and bounds.

However, my love of reading was not to my parents' liking. My father reacted predictably, as I was unavailable at his beck and call. He nicknamed me "O tempelis," the lazy one. My mother would try to yank the books away from my hands; I would have to lock myself in a room upstairs in our hotel to read.

"You'll go blind; you'll go crazy." She would say, sounding sincere as if she wanted to protect me.

Her point of view was simple: she could see no use for books and acted accordingly.

A chasm began separating my family and me very rapidly. Life with my family and the general environment felt very dull to me. Through my reading, I was exposed to another world; I craved improvement and change away from what was around me. I dreamt of a bright future and may have developed attitudinal traits that displeased my family.

Except for my school textbooks, I had to hide somewhere to read other books, like Greek literature, that I borrowed from the Patras library.

I remember once my brother joyfully spending time with a visiting cousin downstairs. I saw them from the partly closed balcony door of the upstairs room where I had locked myself to read. They could not understand why I did not want to join them and "have some fun." But I had lots of fun reading and found the alternative utterly uninteresting.

I kept reading, systematically arranging my knowledge in my mind, and making lists for further reading. I kept notes of sayings and passages I planned to commit to memory. Soon, I had a decent collection and began enjoying showing off my acquired knowledge.

Isn't knowledge fun?

I just wanted to learn! Where is the crime?

Fortunately, a few years later, well into my later teens, I could obtain some primarily European novels and even built a single bookshelf for them in the bedroom. I bound them myself -- an elaborate process. I even wrote the title and author's name on the spine and added an extemporaneous poem on the blank page on the book's cover, front or rear, perhaps just to show off. Years later, my niece Vivi, a good learner, found them and salvaged them for posterity. She offered to return those books during one of my trips to Greece. I chose to take only one, *Christ Recrucified* by Nikos Kazantzakis.

In my parents' Weltanschauung, their world outlook, reading was an exercise that took me away from house and business chores. My father's small businesses – his grocery store, hotel, restaurant, etc., needed workers. What you could do physically mattered; it had immediate value and was easily comprehended by the practical mind. What you could do intellectually was not as easy to appreciate. Scholarship was not on our milieu's menu.

∞∞∞∞

My thirst for reading continued growing, and my writing reflected promising progress. I began composing stories from my imagination during our two-hour biweekly composition class. The teacher delighted in frequently choosing my essay to read in front of my classmates.

Once, however, I was asked, as usual, to read a composition written at home during the Christmas/New Year holidays. It was my most extended piece of writing up to that time. I recall the teacher tapping his right-hand fingers on a student's desk on the first row and now and then looking at me or the distance while I read. I recall an enigmatic smile playing on his face. When I finished, he straightened his torso up, took a deep breath, let out a longish sigh, looked at me, then at the students, again at me, and said:

"You didn't write that story yourself!"

It was an official statement that brooked no objection, no defense. It was final, and I felt crushed. I had worked so hard and expected praise and recognition.

"You couldn't have written it yourself," he continued, driving the nail deeper into my heart.

I wanted to protest and cry and to run away urgently.

"Yes, I did," I objected emphatically, looking him straight in the eyes. "Absolutely, by myself," I added indignantly. The teacher waved his hand away, letting me understand the subject was closed.

Years went by, and the hurt stayed fresh in my heart. It felt like an uncorrected injustice until a new thought hit me one day:

What could have possibly been a better compliment?

The art course

Not all that my parents did was against my educational objectives. Granted, they had to let me finish elementary school as it was obligatory, and willy-nilly, my father allowed me to enter Commercial School. Then, after some astute persuasion, he let me complete it. Yet, an enigmatic exception stands out.

One day, one of our hotel guests noticed some of my artwork on the restaurant wall. It was a painting of the local ferry. There was also a painting by my brother. Our images were far from exquisite; they were fair decorations for otherwise empty walls. Even by the most forgiving impressionistic standards, one could see the artists had a lot to learn. The good thing was that the paintings would frequently lead to a conversation, like once when a customer showed more interest than usual and asked questions. He advised me to cultivate my talent; he informed me there was a correspondence course offered by the Athens Art Academy. He urged me to act on it and said I would not regret it.

∞∞∞∞

The art course idea got planted and deeply rooted in my impressionable mind. I understood if I wanted to progress with my painting, I needed specific instruction. The thought took charge of me. I kept thinking about it and could not sleep. For several days, I felt possessed by the idea. I asked my mother for help to take the course.

"Don't even think about it," she said categorically. "We don't have money to waste." I knew trying to penetrate that kind of wall was a lost battle. I attempted to put the thought away, out of my mind, as it were. But it would not leave. My mother noticed that I would lie in bed, not sleeping. She began worrying about my health. One day, she went up to my father, and I heard her saying:

"John, we'll lose this child; he won't sleep. All he thinks about is this art course."

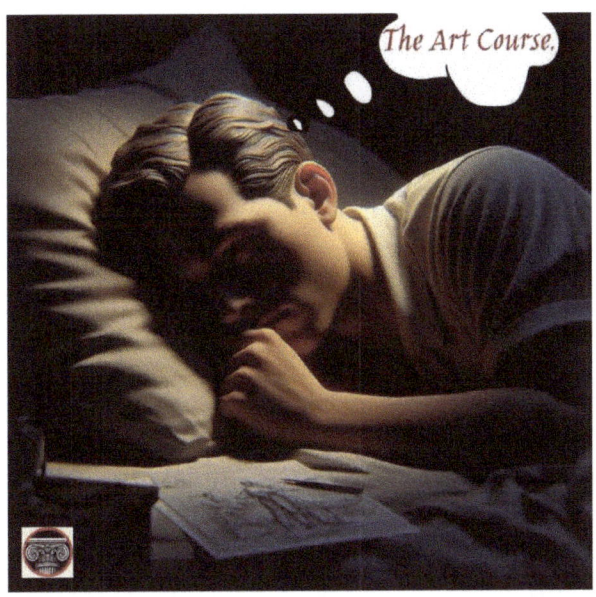

I have no idea how often my parents returned to this topic. Still, some time afterward, I was instructed to find out what the cost of the correspondence course would be. It was not much; it was something my thrifty parents could easily afford. And so, the green light was lit.

Correspondence courses require more ambition and determination than regular classes. I had what it took and finished the course. I was exposed to art perspective – how to represent three-dimensional objects in a two-dimensional plane; I experimented with single and multiple light sources and their effect on shade; I did countless drawings of the human body in various positions and was introduced to water coloring. This was new material for me. I have saved many of those drawings to this day.

That was a good step for my art ambitions. I must go out of my way to show gratitude to my parents, who were able to make this small monetary sacrifice for me despite their education-obstructionist mentality.

Such a small amount of money, so much difference!

Yearning for Music

Music, my love! What a great gift to humanity thou art! People of all times and cultures have loved you; they have listened to you, played, and danced to your magic. Some have even heard you in their dreams. Indeed, you can control our movements and rhythm and even urge us to action. No one needs to teach us how to keep time with any part of our body -- you come built-in.

Where does music come from anyway? Did you ever wonder how it got in us, in our universe?

The songs I heard growing up consisted of what my family members or acquaintances would occasionally sing and what one could listen to during *Panigyria*, Saint Days' festivities. Sometimes, guests of our little Inn would regale the ambiance with a song or two, or an itinerant theater would set up shop across the street for a few performances, including cantata singing. However, with the advent of electricity, the radio became available in my teens and was probably the more reliable source.

I was starved for music.

The minute I would hear someone sing, good or bad, it did not matter; I would pause whatever I was doing and pay attention. Music to me was almost like sunshine to a plant. I would catch myself singing spontaneously, especially in the mornings, evidently a sign of well-being. Indeed, I tend to sing when I feel my best. You probably do, too.

So little music could be heard those days! There was no electricity, and although there were a few radio stations, most people could not afford a radio. Music was needed, especially on Sundays or holidays. People would wear their best clothes and walk up and down the main road in front of Father's stores. My father quickly understood that music was a business tool. People would sit at his restaurant and enjoy some wine with their souvlaki while listening to whatever was on the local station. The inexplicable thing was my father also loved Turkish music! Go figure. He purchased a Grundig radio and a weighty car battery to power it. The problem was the mighty Grundig would eat up a lot of battery power. We had to use it judiciously. Worst of all, taking the heavy battery to Patras by bus was necessary to recharge it as there was no electricity in Rion. And it had to be hand-carried from the bus to the charging station! Then, another trip to get it back -- the darn thing was bulky, and it could leak! Several times, the charging was inadequate, and the trip had to be repeated.

Putting the music source in the same place as me was too tempting. Contrary to my father's strict orders and against his stern admonition, I sometimes waited for everyone to fall asleep before turning the radio on ever so low. With my ear glued to the speaker, I would listen to Italian operas from a Milano station and could not pass up Maria Callas. My father would have skinned me alive had he caught me -- *the radio was needed for the business.* Hardly anyone in our community had the means to listen to music in those days. So starved was I that I could never hear the songs enough to sing them right. There was very little music and a lot of time without it. I missed having enough music when I was growing up.

Now, like anyone, I can listen to music all I want and as many times as I like. I can find the score and the lyrics and play them on my string instruments, but it is almost 70 years too late. On the other hand, perhaps it is not too late -- while I cannot relive my youth, I can still recreate it in my mind.

Childhood is a great time to absorb knowledge and store supportive memories for the future, and isn't music a great accompaniment to our existence? It is with an effort at times that I suppress my envy when I compare my music-deprived childhood to that of others.

Nevertheless, my heart fills up with genuine gratitude that I am still among the living and can enjoy boundless floods of music. What a much better time to be alive!

∞∞∞∞

We all liked to sing in our family. It was one of the few things we could do using our own instruments, our voices. As it did not cost anything, my parents put no obstacles in the way. Occasionally, my father expounded with pride on his grand plan to buy my older sister a violin because she had a great singing voice. It is hard to follow his logic, as the violin would be the last instrument I would pick if I wanted to exploit my good singing voice. His dream never materialized. Every time he mentioned it, it was in a manner that made me feel that I did not merit such a distinction myself or that I was not present or did not exist. This bothered me because I thought otherwise.

On one occasion after dinner, I recall the family sitting at our restaurant while several guests alternated singing their favorite pieces. I must have been about eight or nine at the time. During a brief pause in the general performance, I got up and piped in, singing my uninvited solo in what I thought was my incomparable angelic voice. They all turned to look at me as if I had dropped from the third floor. But they let me finish my song. I recall no comments except for meaningful exchanges of glances. I somehow thought highly of my singing, but I do not remember any positive or negative comments about it from my formative years. I suppose it must have been against the rules to encourage useless talent.

My father prided himself on his singing, and we all used to keep quiet during his occasional solo performances. I cannot say whether it was out of respect or fear. It was how it was done. My mother sang her preferred songs while doing her chores, and sometimes, I would join her.

Singing is one of the things that anyone, rich or poor, can do. It engenders great pleasure and costs nothing. Thus, making music with our built-in instruments, our voices, was OK. Acquiring a musical instrument or aspiring to be a musician, on the other hand, was frowned upon. No amount of begging could persuade either of my parents to allow it.

∞∞∞

My attempts to acquire and learn how to play an instrument had been rather heroic. I had no money whatsoever. Everyone in the family worked, adults and children, but all the money belonged to my father. The children had no allowance, and even the concept was unknown. Tipping was not the custom in our restaurant in those disadvantaged times, and although the till was always available, I never took a drachma.

However, one needs money to purchase a musical instrument! My frequent begging for a cheap, beaten-up string instrument like a mandolin, a guitar, or a bouzouki elicited a decisive and unequivocal "No." I resolved that if my parents were not buying me an instrument, I would get one myself. I had to find an honest way to put some money together. So, I thought up my "business plan."

According to long-standing tradition, a couple of times a year, around the Christmas holidays, children would go from house to house singing carols ("Kalanda.") Even the poorest homes would open their doors and allow the children to sing the tradition-prescribed carols. It had to be done early in the morning according to tradition. As per my grand plan, I decided to go alone to avoid having to share the yield. No one complained if I woke them up; I recall people patiently listening to my rendition and giving me a few coins at the conclusion.

Thus, I accumulated my small drachma bundle and began looking for any musical instrument. Word of mouth was the only way, as I was unaware of any classifieds. Eventually, someone who knew someone in Patras turned up who had an old beaten-up accordion lying around the house. A few keytops were missing; otherwise, it could produce a sound.

However, the price was more than I could afford: 80 drachmas! I only had 60. The owner, a young fellow with no use for music but in whose house this lonesome instrument was languishing, agreed to let me take it for 60 drachmas upfront and the remainder from the proceeds of the following calendar round.

I brought the heavy instrument home one evening with great anticipation and trepidation. Using the back entrance, I surreptitiously placed it under the bed while trying to figure out my next step. I was proud of myself and filled with joy. I had planned and executed the required steps to a tee. I now had my instrument, but I was not counting on the *deus ex machina.*

When I returned from school the next day, the instrument was lying outside in the side yard – my mother had let it slide out of the window, causing more damage!

NO ACCORDIONS IN MY HOUSE!

One can catalog all sorts of parental cruelty. How would you classify this one? I cried bitter tears. A couple more keys were now broken. My mother was categorical: she would not allow any instrument in her house. I was directed to return it immediately, which I did. Still, I could not recover all my investment due to the damage my mother had caused.

You probably wonder whether I hate my mother. Not really. I could never hate her or anyone, which has been a blessing; I preferred to put my energies elsewhere. Like most parents, mine evidently had definite ideas about how to direct their children's future success. They followed their values, as they were genuinely principled people in their strange way.

What does it mean to be principled? It means adhering to rules the group members understand, accept, and aspire to. A child growing up in a family absorbs such rules or principles the same way it grows up speaking the mother tongue – it is part of the environment. A child cannot question these "principles" while growing up any more than it could challenge the grammatical structure of the mother tongue.

But it felt awful and unfair that my mother would not allow a musical instrument in the house. Our society did not forbid it, as other families had musical instruments to play, sing, and dance with at home. It did not make sense to me; I could see no harm in it; besides, it felt so good to create music. However, as I had no choice, I succumbed, and life, such as it was, went on.

I have said I did not hate my mother despite it all. But did I love her?

∞∞∞∞

Nonetheless, my mother's or anyone's orders could not extinguish my desire to acquire an instrument. In fact, my parents' obstacles strengthened it. I wanted, nay, I needed to play an instrument!

When I was about 15, my musical luck began favoring me. On a visit to my uncle Elias' house, I spotted an old mandolin. No one in his house was interested in playing it. As it had been collecting dust, he agreed to loan it to me.

I brought the mandolin home with great trepidation. Remembering the accordion's fate a few years earlier and knowing what to expect, I approached my mother directly. Holding the instrument with reverence, I admonished her not to throw it out because it belonged to my uncle, her favorite brother. Unbelievable as it may sound, she let me put it in our bedroom. She did not interfere further until one day when she came upon some of our merry-making.

My siblings and a young soldier serving in a nearby military base were circle dancing in our back room while I played some traditional Greek songs, which I had figured out by ear. My mother got furious, yanked the mandolin off my hands, and chased everybody away. I was afraid she would throw the instrument out the window. I protested we had done nothing wrong and begged her to give me the mandolin back. Eventually, she did later, and I could occasionally practice until one fateful night.

Several customers were at the restaurant that night, and I decided to show off my mandolin virtuosity. As I was getting ready to play, my younger sister, Chrisanthi, suddenly grabbed the instrument out of my hands for some reason. I tried to get it back, and it fell to the floor, causing the neck to break. I was disconsolate. My first and only "allowed" instrument, my uncle's mandolin, got broken! Absolute disaster had struck.

Was I destined never to have a musical instrument?

∞∞∞∞

Sometime later, while I was still a student at the Patras Commercial School, our ever-enterprising principal decided to form a school band. He procured the necessary funds, went to Italy, returned with a dozen wind instruments, and hired a musician. It was announced with great pomp that anyone from the six classes could try out.

With hope burning in my heart, I thought the time had finally come and that my parents could not object as there was no cost to them, and this was a sanctioned course. Without telling them, I applied and was among the dozen finalists.

I went to the first lesson. As I recall, the teacher presented some basic music concepts, like the pentagram and musical notes. I gobbled it all up with a voracious appetite. I returned to the next class with a simple, note-by-note transcription of "Aigiotisa," Lady from Aigion, a traditional Greek song. After class, I showed it to the teacher, anxiously hungry for approval. The teacher was impressed. He asked me who wrote it, made minor corrections, and assumed I had had music lessons. Mind you, I am not a musical genius. I applied the teacher's first pentagram and octave instructions to a well-known and simple melody. I was excited to return home and tell my people of my musical success.

That was a grave mistake, as I found out later.

The teacher took me aside the next time before our third music lesson started and said he was sorry.

"Your lips are too thick for wind instruments." He explained. Mind you, the school had not yet received the instruments, and I had not had the chance to try them! I was crestfallen, going from some kind of musical euphoria to nothing. Years later, I discovered that many people with very "thick lips," considerably thicker than mine, have no problem playing wind instruments. The funny part is that I never suspected a familial *deus ex machina* until now. Had my father or mother paid a visit to the school's principal?

I sometimes wonder where our interests come from and why some are more persistent than others. Playing a musical instrument was a matter of pleasure and enjoyment. I perceived creating music as a fun activity coupled with some natural aptitude. I never considered it a means to make a living, although I felt it was one way to impress others and distinguish myself.

Interests vary and change from time to time. Other factors interfere with changing their course. We may be unaware of such things. However, *strong interests* tend to persevere.

∞∞∞∞

My revenge: my mother's obstacle course has had the opposite effect. I cannot compare my playing with that of great guitarists, but I managed to learn how to play both classical pieces and popular songs on a guitar. I even dabbled with the bouzouki. As I track people I have known through my mind, I find primarily *would-be* instrument players. Few people continue playing, including those who had every opportunity and encouragement. There are so many lonely instruments in homes all over. You may have some yourself or know someone who does as you read this.

My parents lamentably succeeded in preventing me from getting a formal musical education. Still, they could not extinguish my great love for music.

When I was about seventeen, after my father would no longer "dare" beat me, I got a job as a waiter at a beach restaurant. I gave my father most of the money but kept some for a smallish, beat-up guitar and some books. I got the notes for "La Paloma," a well-known Latin American tune. I started figuring things out by ear and logical analysis of musical notes. No teacher. I managed to put together a recognizable performance, which I play somewhat better now.

One day, I demonstrated "my achievement" to my parents. I remember them looking on, unimpressed, without any comments. To say that I did not understand my parents' persecution of my musical explorations would be incorrect; they had made that abundantly clear repeatedly.

"Musicians are always poor. They earn very little. Do you want a life like that?"

One cannot deny the merits of their argument. Setting aside the self-interest implications, they believed that, as parents, they were doing the best for their offspring. In their pragmatically sterile understanding of their world, there was no room for art as a source of enjoyment because everything had to do with money and how to put food on the table. That was the overriding criterion forced upon them by their place in their war-plagued times. It was a philosophy born by circumstances.

It is not infrequent that choices are made for us, like an accident, an aberrant individual, a war, etc., agents outside our control. No matter how sober and vigilant a life we may lead, events may affect us, changing the course of our lives. Although I do not allow such concerns to rule my life, it is precisely such factors that I fear.

One may have an innate desire to play a musical instrument or learn a foreign language. The obstacle is the required learning effort. If it were possible to purchase and install that knowledge, wouldn't most people want it? When the desire is strong, the individual finds the way.

Life is replete with unpredictabilities; it is a long road sprinkled with choices, some created by us and some by others. Then, there are the consequences of past decisions, whether made by us or others.

I regret that I was not allowed to receive a formal musical education. There was a time for this, and I was more than ready. There is no point blaming my parents or even the circumstances. Some things we do not get to choose. However, I envy those offered the opportunity in their childhood to pick up the coveted knowledge, cultivate it, and possess it all their lives. I imagine all my half-hearted attempts to acquire that knowledge by hook or crook have not amounted to what otherwise could have been.

Still, I must be content and grateful for what life has permitted me to accomplish with my musical appetite. Later, I found ways to make music a companion for life.

A dynamite of dynamism

I read an article in our local paper about a retired Greek-American who had returned to Greece with a plan to build a school in his mountain birthplace in central Greece. The year was 1957, and the village was located a few hours by bus from Rion. I took note of the date of the inauguration, and I hitched a ride on a truck and went there. I met the man, and more memorably, I met the Athenian journalist who had written the article and had been following the thread of his story. I immediately connected with the journalist; he was impressed with my initiative and ambition. I had gone there to persuade the education-supportive Greek American to help me emigrate to America.

The wise journalist sized me up and down; he agreed to let me ride with him back to Rion on his way to Athens and even volunteered to warn me about a trait of mine. I was impressed with his perspicacity and jotted his words down right there and then:

« Ἔχεις δυναμισμό μέσα σου.” You have dynamism inside you, he said. And he continued: "Try to devote yourself to one thing exclusively. You love books; dedicate yourself to them if you listen to me. Beware of distractions because you are the kind of person who devotes himself to what he does, who allows his dynamism to take over."

Great advice. Did I follow it?

The Jewish elopement

As with paying for the art course, my parents showed other benevolent aspects of their character. They did not discriminate racially, were not ethnically prejudiced, and could frequently be helpful. My father would readily invite passers-by to our dinner table and treat them to our best.

This was in the early fifties. I must have been about fifteen years old. This was the time I fancied presenting myself to the world as the greatest novelist since Kazanzakis. I volunteered to stay up nights manning our little hotel and using the quiet time to write the novel to end all novels. I must have been well into my third chapter when, with midnight already behind me, a knock on the door took me away from a belabored detail of my magnum opus. A young man was standing at the threshold.

"Kalispera" (Good evening), he muttered as unsure a twenty-something could ever be, addressing a 15-year-old. "I, we need a room." I looked for the "we" part and noticed an uncertain female silhouette blending into the night's darkness behind him.

"How many of you are there?"

"Just two, my fiancée and myself."

I invited them into the hall and proceeded to write down their names.

"I can't tell you my fiancée's name," he muttered.

"I am afraid we need to have it. Is there any reason why we can't have it?"

"Hm, … we just eloped," he said as if that were an established reason not to give one's name.

I led them to their room and returned to my scribbling.

The following day came, and the day after that. The young couple continued their sojourn at our little hotel. It did not take long to get to know their whole story. They were desperate. He told me he was Jewish but was willing to marry in the Greek Orthodox Church because he loved the girl and religion was not important to him. However, the girl's parents did not want her to marry the man. He did not say whether his Jewishness had anything to do with it.

At any rate, the Greeks of my time, and to my knowledge, did not discriminate against Jews the way other nationalities do. I grew up not having the slightest sense of prejudice against Jews. I did not even know there were Jews in our community. It was not a factor; it did not matter. We all had one national identity: we were all Greeks.

The appearance of our Jewish guest, however, raised my curiosity, and I recall asking my father what he thought about Jews.

"They're smart businessmen." He said. That is all I ever got out of him on the subject.

The young man confessed he did not have much money and did not know what to do. I shared his plight with my mother.

"Do they want to get married?" she wanted to know.

"Yes."

"OK, we'll help them. I still have my Stefana. And I can also loan them my wedding rings," was my mother's unhesitating practical solution.

The Stefana are two crowns or wreaths that are placed on the couple's heads and are exchanged three times during the ceremony to signal the ceremony has the protection of the Holy Trinity -- Father, Son, and Holy Spirit. The ribbon symbolizes the couple's unity and commitment to each other in the Greek Orthodox social and religious context.

I thought this was the time to collect from our community's priest. In my younger years, I acted as his altar boy for a long time, helping to open the church and do other tasks, including occasionally reciting the "Pater imon" (Our Father – The Lord's Prayer).

The wedding ceremony was set for the following day. I served as the Best Man. The young couple got married and went on their way. We got the job done. The priest, however, was not happy with the sum I paid him and dunned me for more money for some time afterward.

My friend George informed me the couple had a child a few years later. I was hurt and disappointed they did not follow the custom as I understood it. As the Best Man, I was supposed to become the child's Godfather and participate in the choice of a name. Although I lived a few blocks from them, they chose not to follow the custom or associate with me. You see, I was a poor language tutor then.

C'est la vie.

Onassis to the rescue?

In my quest for a way out of Greece, I did not forget Aristotle Onassis. He represented the quintessential Greek expatriate success story. For Greeks, he was a living god. On his way to becoming one of the world's wealthiest men and marrying Jackie Kennedy, the widow of John F. Kennedy, President of the United States, he had overcome many difficulties, some of which were life-threatening!

I sent Onassis a handwritten letter requesting work in any of his businesses. I stated my language background and that I possessed my Ναυτικό Βιβλιάριο, a Navy Booklet, which meant I could work on a ship. I never got an answer. He must have received many such offers from impressionable and enthusiastic people. Chances are, he never saw my letter himself. Later in my life, after achieving some success, I received comparable proposals from people wishing to work for me. I even received capital offers from people who wanted to invest in my business success. But I answered them all, unlike Onassis, as there were not too many.

Australia, here I come!

Rumors were buzzing all around that Australia had opened its gates for unlimited Greek emigration in the mid-fifties. Australia, about the same size as the continental USA, had only about 9.5 million people at that time. It needed people to support its economic development. Its post-Second World War "Populate or Perish" policy encouraged immigration from several countries, including Greece. By the thousands, Greeks jumped at this unique opportunity to improve their economic prospects.

Feeling the inexorable pace of elapsing time as I was one year away from high school graduation and seriously doubting my family's commitment to my education, I went to the Australian consulate in Patras. It was a small, no-frills, one-room office manned by a single person, who by all appearances was Greek.

Right away, I tried my English as I was eager to show the kind of person I was. The man was impressed and responded in heavily accented English while quickly slipping into Greek. He asked where I had learned English and what he could do for me. I told him plainly that I sought better opportunities. Naturally, I could not say I wanted to get an education, as that was not what his office was engaged in.

"How old are you?" He fired his first question as if reading it from a prepared script.

"Almost seventeen," I said, puffing my chest like a frigate bird. I knew Australia was looking for workers, and physical size was a factor. I feared my short frame would disqualify me.

"How much schooling have you had?" he asked, looking me over like a merchandise article.

"Almost done with high school; one year to go."

He paused for a minute, glanced at some paper on his desk, and figured he was done with his questions.

"Come back next year after you finish your schooling," he said calmly.

I thought his advice was reasonable and felt I had put myself on a career path for Australia.

Sweden, take me in!

On a different occasion, I happened to be at the port of Patras. Several ships were anchored at the pier. As I walked past a cargo ship flying the Swedish flag, I stepped up the gangway as if I belonged there, entirely without thinking and on impulse. A sailor intercepted me at the top of the gangplank.

"I need to speak to the captain," I said confidently in English.

"You can't do that," he responded, putting his arms up and pushing me slightly backward.

"I really need to see the *captain*," I insisted. "Please," I continued.

The man looked at me as if measuring me up and decided to do me a favor, probably because I spoke in English.

"Wait here." He said.

A few minutes later, a tall, middle-aged, blondish North European approached me.

"What can I do for you?" the captain asked patiently.

"I have my Navy Booklet," I said. "Besides Greek, I can speak English, French, and Italian. I am a good worker. I want to work on your boat."

He looked at me briefly and then said:

"I am very sorry. The laws of your country don't allow me to employ you," and raising his arms outward, palms up, waist-high to show helplessness, he continued: "Besides, I don't need more workers on this boat. Very sorry!"

He looked frank and non-engaging, as non-Greeks generally do. I thanked him and took my leave.

Selling to sailors

America's Sixth Fleet, established in 1950, was based in the Mediterranean. I recall seeing a large ship of this fleet anchored offshore of Rion, my birthplace. Sailors were allowed ashore to explore and mix with the locals; they "invaded" our grocery shop as well as the competitor's, anxious to buy alcohol. Our little store had some bottled wine, and there was also wine made by my father, which was stored in giant vats at our storage facility behind the main structure. As is well-known, Greece has been making good wines for a long time (what do you expect? After all, wasn't it Greek wine that inebriated Cyclops?)

My father wasted no time raising the price of his wine; our meager supply was exhausted in a few hours. More significantly, it was the first time he saw me in English language action.

And he liked what he saw very much.

He dispatched me to Patras to buy a sizable supply of bottled wine and, placing a dozen bottles in a wicker picnic basket, commanded me to go to the beach near the anchored ship to peddle wine. I obliged and managed to sell my supply quickly using my English. The next day, the process was repeated till the boat was gone. And again when the ships returned.

One can become a slave to one's competence.

Chances are my father's eyes were opened wider than wide, realizing what a valuable commodity I could be. He saw another opportunity to exploit me between Sixth Fleet ship moorings. He proposed that I sell chestnuts on the Rion-Antirrion ferry! I put my foot down. I was not going to do that! Was he out of his mind? Did he want to humiliate me?

My knowledge of English was in danger of becoming an obstacle to my education. And so was my ability to sell.

And would you blame my father if he did not want to lose such a valuable and free employee? If you are shocked considering family exploitation, please do not be. Child labor laws are a recent phenomenon. Even at a very young age, children's work has been a legitimate source of additional family income and is still an accepted practice in many countries.

4. Leaving Home Once

Faustian bargain

With improved incomes after the war, people from Patras began looking for a summer vacation spot. Rion, my birthplace, became fashionable as an excellent summer place. It was conveniently close -- only about seven kilometers away. The sea wind from either side of the cape was largely dependable – it kept summer temperatures much cooler than in Patras. The beach was relatively unspoiled – the world's longest fully-suspended Rion-Antirrion Bridge and the colossal motorway were far into the future. Rion was then, and probably still is, a great spot to swim and have lunch at one of its many beach cafes.

Our immediate community had only one grocery store, which was located across from my father's establishments. With the increased summer population, my father saw an opportunity to open his own grocery store. In the spring of 1956, when I was completing commercial school, my father announced his decision to the family: my brother and I were to set up and manage the grocery store. I was now the most educated member of the family, as my brother, older than me, was encouraged to quit after his second year at commercial school. I was expected by my education to take the lead. It was at this juncture that I saw an auspicious opening.

"I can guarantee the store is a success," I told my father. "We can make a lot of money, but I do not see the use of having me around here in the winter. If you help me study in Italy in the winter, I will make you a lot of money in the summer. I only need a $30 monthly loan from you while studying. I will work hard to make the store a huge success in the summertime. As for the loan, I will repay you after completing my studies and getting a job. And I'm willing to pay interest."

I must have surprised my father, but he knew I was serious. It was a good deal, and he risked nothing by accepting my proposal. After considering it for a while, he agreed. This was our oral agreement between father and son. The 30-dollar monthly sum was considered the absolute minimum for a thrifty student without knowing the Italian cost of living. As I did not know how to cook, my mother agreed to teach me how to prepare a few inexpensive basic meals. All was set.

∞∞∞∞

We were all expected to work. No family member earned any money from their work. It all went to my father. Even the money I made outside his employment, such as when I served as a waiter in a beachfront restaurant, went mainly to him as a moral duty.

That is what a good son was expected to do.

There were a lot of chores. In my father's mind, there was only work. We never took a vacation. Never! We were to be available 24/7 if necessary. The neighbor's store had store hours. Not my father's. Anyone could knock on the side door any time, and we would oblige.

∞∞∞∞

We were looking forward to a profitable summer and were fully aware business would dry up after the summer months. As a grocery delivery service had never been offered in our community, my brother and I planned to go door to door every morning. We would gather orders and then make deliveries. For this, some wheels were necessary; there was no question about getting a car in those days, as private car ownership was extremely rare. All we would need and could obtain would be a bicycle.

We figured out what the next step would be. One of our customers had a smith shop in the industrial part of Patras. We worked out a design for fabricating side-by-side metal baskets for the bicycle. Of course, plastic was in the far future. The baskets were connected and placed over the bicycle's rear seat. A reasonable plan, except I thought the good smith had made them very heavy. As my father had never ridden a cycle, he did not feel my objection had merit -- imagine a 30-plus-lbs. bike, loaded with a 20-pound metal basket plus whatever groceries were to be delivered. A lot of strength was required, especially going uphill; one would tire quickly. I did make the point to my father, but it did not help.

Post-war bicycles, including what was left behind from the war, were heavy and made of iron. Weight was not on people's minds. What mattered was strength. Bicycles were workhorses. Even today, one can see inventive uses of bicycles in third-world countries, marveling at the number and size of different things crammed onto this versatile two-wheeled horse.

Every morning, I would gather orders door-to-door and return to the store. While I was filling them out, my brother would use the bicycle to get orders from a somewhat smaller territory. We were doing great, and my father was happy. This was a perfect situation for him. His gratuitous assistants were proving as productive as can be -- we were part of his well-oiled machine. My father was not the only one happy with the situation. So was I. I had his promise to continue my education at the end of the summer after the vacationers were gone. I had hypnotized myself into an all-out effort and managed to function at maximum capacity. The customers liked me as I never hesitated to go the extra mile. And I never missed an opportunity to proudly bend any willing ear with my plans for higher education.

I worked hard for my customers, sometimes until very late in the day; I would even sit and wait after hours at a beach restaurant to get grocery orders. One incident stands out. A summer evening, Katina Paxinou -- the famous Greek actress who portrayed Pilar in Hemingway's "For Whom the Bell Tolls" -- came to my customer's beach restaurant. Mind you, there were no phones in general use then -- only one phone for the entire suburban community. The restauranteur asked me to stand by until the actress' company could decide what to have for dinner. I got my order for groceries and rushed to fill it, riding my bicycle at top speed through a vineyard shortcut during a dark, star-less night. Our grocery store was some 15 bicycle minutes away.

∞∞∞∞

As I hated to have my customers wait, I always felt rushed when filling orders. I cannot explain that. Even nowadays, I dislike wasting time, mine or somebody else's.

One day, as I turned a sharp corner going downhill at a higher speed, I lost control of the heavily loaded bicycle. My bicycle slid to the ground, and the orders scattered all over. Unperturbed, I began picking up the stuff as fast as possible. My legs were badly scratched, and some blood was flowing. And my right arm was not doing much better. However, I had to make the deliveries on time – people needed to get going with their cooking. Out of nowhere, I saw my father hurrying towards me, his face filled with sincere concern. I would prefer to believe it was for my welfare.

Accidental delivery.

«Τι έγινε μωρέ παιδί μου;» (What happened, my boy?) Evidently, someone had seen my plight and had alerted him.

Whether going the super extra mile or hurting myself maneuvering the heavy delivery bicycle, a flame kept burning brightly inside me:

I was earning my education.

Readying for Italy

Since things were going well that summer and my parents were satisfied, I thought of pushing my luck a bit. With great difficulty, I persuaded my mother to let me have a few Italian language lessons in exchange for something I no longer remember. I found an Italian lady who tutored her language – she was married to a Greek. Moreover, she offered to come to Rion at no extra charge – she regarded that as her summer beach outing. Before connecting with her, I had been using an Italian self-teaching method.

The poor lady looked at me in awe one day after our lesson. She remained silent momentarily; she clearly wanted to say something, but the words would not come out. Finally, she uttered "ftou, ftou," a form of quasi-spitting, as done in some cultures, to ward off evil spirits. "Go hang an amulet around your neck," she said. At first, I was not sure I understood. Then, she explained how impressed she was with how much I had learned quickly. She went on to say her son could not learn in years what I had learned after a few lessons.

Even my father was impressed!

Father's betrayal

Recall the deal: my father had agreed to loan me 30 dollars monthly to study in Italy in exchange for my helping to set up and run the grocery store during the peak season without any salary. I kept my end of the bargain and more. I even worked part-time as a waiter for a restaurant at the ferry boat pier and gave most of the money to my father.

At the end of the summer, I went to the Italian embassy in Athens as planned. I prepared my passport and the necessary documents in Greek and obtained the official translation in Italian. (I still have those papers!) It was on Tuesday, and I was to leave on a Thursday. I came back from Athens ready to proceed as planned.

"You're not going anywhere," -- my father's bombshell pierced my hearing. "We need you here. We must marry your sisters off first -- we must save money for their dowries, and you need to do your military service. After that, you can do your university studies." That was the old depressing, oppressive, dispiriting mantra. I was devastated!

My father, my own father, my very own father, had deceived me big time!

I was unimaginably disappointed and in great despair. It feels awful to get conned any time and worse if your own father has done the swindling. He was expected to be my moral guide but had tricked me. How could I ever trust him again?

Lamentably, the rest of the family unanimously supported his decision.

I tried hard to get my father to change his mind. I contacted a customer from our community, an engineer my father respected and to whose house I delivered groceries regularly during the summer season. I was under the impression he was on my side. I implored him to use whatever influence he had to change my father's mind in my favor. He promised he would. I waited anxiously until we met at the railroad tracks across from my father's establishment a few days later.

"Your father is right," he said categorically. "Your help is needed to marry off your sisters. After you do your military duty, you can pursue your studies." He was repeating my father's line.

What was I thinking asking this man for help? I could not comprehend how he had come to agree with my father. I have no idea what his reasons were. But his response was a devastating mystery to me. Much later, it occurred to me that he, too, was a victim of the culture: you must help with the sisters' dowry and serve in the military; you must obey your parents and be ready to do your all for family honor. You must …

Itinerant Despair

Disillusioned and disgusted by my father's broken promise, I started looking for a job. Jobs were tough to come by; it was mostly a function of who you knew. Unable to find any other job, I agreed to sell door-to-door subscriptions for the blind. It was a periodical based on the claim that the money or part of it would go toward helping the blind. I never learned if it did and had no way at that time to find out. I needed to do something to survive and get away from the colossal disappointment my father turned out to be.

I worked door-to-door for several months, wearing the same pair of pants and whatever I had on my back when I left. I remember how cold it was and how I would carefully place my pants under my pillow every night to maintain the crease. A crease was thought to be neat at the time. Along with a young man from Piraeus, we covered a substantial part of north-central Greece, which I journaled in detail. I have saved the journal to this day.

Wherever we went, I made it a point to inform myself of the historical sights. I visited as many archeological places as possible - - Greece is so full of history. I was interested in learning. That must have distinguished me from many of my contemporaries. I had a few books with me, which I read avidly.

My partner was an ill-bred young man with bad habits. He was street-savvy and never read anything; he smoked, gambled, and managed to "borrow" small sums a couple of times from me and never repaid. Months after we stopped working together, I visited his mother in Piraeus and found out he was in jail.

Cold forced me to arrange to get some of my garments from my family. An acquaintance would be passing by Rion, and he offered to help. My parents refused to hand over any of my clothes, however. I was freezing. I remember once on an unheated bus in winter with snow covering the ground, pressing my back against the bus seat to keep warm. All I had on me was a tee shirt, a shirt, and a light autumn coat. I remember the penetrating cold as if it were yesterday.

I also had my cheap little guitar with me, and occasionally, I would play on the bus with people chiming in and singing traditional songs.

Faustian bargain renewed

1956 turned into 1957, and I called the family home from Northern Greece, feeling homesick. I had missed the only family I had. My diary shows how I had a genuine love for them. I got my father on the phone.

«Που εισαι μωρε παιδι μου?» "Where are you, my boy?" He was glad to hear from me and showed surprising interest in my well-being. He asked me to come home without delay. I told him I would return only if we could renew our agreement; I would help him with his grocery store for another summer if he would support my study in Italy. He readily agreed.

"Do you mean it?" I managed to ask, remembering his betrayal.

"Yes," he responded most emphatically.

And so it was that I returned home on March 1, 1957, after a six-month absence. I had forgiven my father for his betrayal. He was thrilled to see me. To show his joy, he did something he had never done before for me: he prepared a delicacy, calf's brain a la grecque.

I was hoping to be at an Italian campus in the fall, with only the loss of one year to reconcile. It bothered me greatly that time was going by without advancing my education. The urgent feeling that I did not have much time made me tense and unhappy. Time was to be used efficiently and wisely – this was part of my make-up. I was born with this programmed instruction.

5. Leaving Home Again

eet the maid

Meet the maid
Soon, disagreements began, my father's usual abuse resumed, and I did my best to ignore it all and keep the peace. One can endure a great deal for a worthwhile goal. The summer came, and I worked harder than ever, knowing my education was at stake. And I made my father good money.

As if the work days were not long enough, I thought of doing some uninterrupted studying before falling asleep. I put a small mattress on the low-pitched barn roof and used a flashlight to work on my Italian.

Rion had become a relaxed suburb for summer vacationers. Well-to-do Patras families would rent several rooms and bring their maidservants along. Olympia, one of the maids, an attractive twenty-year-old, noticed where I slept on the barn roof. Right across from my roof spot was the main building, our hotel. One of the hotel restrooms was at the building's end and close to the barn. The barn and the hotel were separate structures.

Olympia became exceedingly preoccupied with the cleanliness of the restroom; she would show her face through the small bathroom window, exhibiting "disinterested" interest the way only interested women can do. The end of the summer was approaching, and the rest is history, as they say. Nature took over, and we found our way toward brief intimacy without anyone finding out.

Father's second betrayal

At summer's end, following the agreed-upon plan to study in Italy, I gathered my passport and relevant papers just like I had done the year before. I did not forget the simple meal cooking notes made from consulting with my mother. I was filled with excitement and anticipation: I would be on Italian soil studying at an Italian university in about a week!

However, as only the devil could have willed it, my father released the same old cannonball a few days before my departure.

"You're not going now. We'll marry off your sisters first, and after your military service, you can go."

Hell broke loose.

Father had deceived me again!

He failed to keep his promise to support my university studies after exploiting me during the peak season for the second time around.

Would you do this to your own child?

Tradition orders priorities its own way. Dowry for unmarried siblings trumped education. Support for education paled by comparison -- any reasonable community member would see that my father was doing the "right thing." But they would not know of his deceit. Or, they would condone it because the cause was for the sake of tradition. And they would be oblivious to the profundity of my pain, the agony of a youth fighting for his education. There was no court of justice for my plight.

I was a victim without defense.

Frothing at the mouth, the exchange with my father was at its ugliest ever. I left the house and walked to the beach to mull things over.

Beat and ban

I'm returning home from a long walk on the beach. I'm trying to clear my befogged mind, figure out what to do, and sort things out.

My father told me this morning to forget about my education. No Italy, no university, no future. My father deceived me for the second time. Our deal is dead.

I lost who I was, forsaken with a blurred horizon and without a compass and adrift. I am a man without a dream.

I am approaching our home, the only home I have ever known. I see them, my father, mother, two sisters, and brother, all sitting around the family table. I hear them talking, animated as usual.

"Να κι' ο τεμπέλης μας," (Here comes our lazy one,) says my father with his self-satisfied sarcasm. I enter the house and approach the dinner table.

Like a swarm of maddened bees, they all descend upon me. Slaps and fists are raining on me. I raise my arms to protect myself from this inexplicable and unexpected avalanche of collective cruelty. Such has never happened before. I beat a hasty retreat. I run outside around the back of the house like a hunted animal.

Wasn't it enough that Father had deceived me? Did they have to beat me up to boot?

Those whom you love the most can hurt the most.

I reach the back of the house; my mother and brother already have anticipated my next move. My mother is standing at the bottom of the stairs leading up to the hotel. My brother is at her right and a bit behind. Their menacing expressions leave no doubt as to their determination.

"Get out of here!" my mother fires her first shot. I beg her to let me take some personal things. "Leave, or I call the police now."

"Please!" I implore them.

My brother, like a Roman centurion, is now moving closer. He blocks my way.

He was bigger than me and had already tasted "blood" after participating in my common thrashing a few minutes ago.

I cannot believe this is happening. I cannot believe this is happening. I cannot believe this is happening! I am given no choice. My family, my mother and my brother, are doing this. My mind cannot fathom it. There is no alternative; this is the end!

They would not let me take anything, clothes or personal things. My mother threatened to call the police, and she meant it. As only the worst of luck would have it, the police lived upstairs in a room at Father's hotel, one flight of stairs away, the closest distance from any other house in all of Rion! I had no choice.

I turn around and grab an old, discarded bicycle lying against the barn wall. I am riding the old bike, headed uphill. I am pedaling hard. My eyes are filled with tears, and my vision is blurred. I am suffocating. I have no idea what to do. I am not wanted; I have been tossed out.

I was rejected. Completely and with irrefutable finality. My father deceived me for the second time! My family has cheated me of my education and life's dream.

Where am I going? I do not know. I am getting away from somewhere, from someone, from something. I am crossing a dividing line, entering a one-way road, and leaving my past behind.

I am pushed to something else, to a fathomless, unknown chasm. I am filled with negativism and growing despair.

My own people were destroying me because I wanted an education.

I no longer feel hungry. The gushing tears have by now dried up. I hear the bicycle frame squeak with every turn of the crank and recall why we had not used it. What if the cracked frame breaks as I am going fast downhill? Never mind! I have got worse issues to deal with.

What do I do now?

You shall regret it!

I reached Patras, utterly confused, with my heart brimming with the worst misery, gloom, and desolation I had ever felt in my entire life. I did not have any money, not a penny! All alone, penniless, homeless, and hopeless, with my education dream nullified.

Where am I to spend the night? Where can I go? I ride past Uncle Elias' neighborhood and ride on; I don't feel close enough to bother him with my problems.

I round the vast cemetery and feel envious of the dead. I am in a haze. My thoughts are in a storm. There is no clarity.

"Room for rent." I see a sign on the opposite side of the road. Zombie-like, I turn into a modest neighborhood. I knock on the door. An agreeable-looking, middle-aged lady opens the door and receives me with a smile. We talk about the room rent. I tell her I have no money now but hope to get a job soon. She shows me the room. It's a small room. There's a bed with a mattress on it – no pillow or sheets. I take it and settle in. I have nothing except the clothes on my back and the old bicycle.

The lady explained the rules, but I was having difficulty concentrating.

"You can stay here, starting now," she tells me. I nod, and she leaves the small room, shutting the door. I lie on the mattress right away with all my clothes on. I look at the low ceiling and struggle to push the fog away. I am supposed to be on my way to Italy in a couple of days. I have been telling everybody about this with pride and joy for months, and look at me now. So, I have been lying to all those people. What a shame!

I quash my tears as best as possible; I do not want anyone to hear me through the flimsy door. There is no going back; I am entirely on my own.

You shall regret it, all of you, I promise!

Adieu, my family

Did my family hate me, or did they simply not love me? They acted as if they did both. With the summer demand for my services now absent, I was an annoying presence to them, a reminder of broken promises.

I do not think it's accurate to say that my family hated me. I need to believe they did not. Still, I must concede their actions showed a total lack of love and basic empathy. What happened that day was an infamous act, a shameful act. I have been able to forgive them all without any difficulty because I am blessedly unable to hate.

But I have not been able to forget.

Knowing the lack of job opportunities, my father likely thought I would crawl back, begging to be admitted under his tent. He would say as much repeatedly. Little did he know the magnitude of my pride and the depth of my resolve.

I was determined to die than go back.

This may sound like an exaggeration or Hellenic histrionics. Still, it was undoubtedly an accurate state of mind and remained so.

Why the banning?

Was this herd mentality? Why did my family treat me this way? Granted, they must have perceived me as strange and unusual, not fitting the mold. Would it be too self-serving if I stated that mediocrity loves company and abhors excellence because it senses it cannot attain it? The family's treatment of me was not a conscious reaction. I wanted to become better than I was and better than they were; I yearned to achieve excellence, to amount to something big.

I had myself to impress.

I was infected with ambition and was super-thirsty for success. And I may have been a bit impatient; I may even have been arrogant and off-putting. And I may have rubbed my relatives the wrong way. But I was also solicitous and caring. Admittedly, I preferred to study and disliked chores, but I did them. I toed the line. And I gave them my all in the two summers, as agreed.

I was becoming aware of my worth. And it may not have been good to let it be shown. How can a teenager know how to control natural emotions? Is wisdom ever not in short supply?

∞∞∞∞

The dictatorial father rules. My brother, sisters, and mother quickly followed Father's lead and even led. How could the whole family show such a remarkable lack of empathy toward me? Did some kind of madness rob them of their common sense? One thing is indisputable: they feared my father. Where did fraternal and maternal love go?

My sisters, prisoners of a traditional Greek family, had little choice. They depended totally on my parents' support and goodwill, especially my autocrat of a father. His word was law. They could not possibly do anything to annoy him; they had to tread around him with caution. And he could be cruel. Truthfully, he was not as mean to them as he was with us boys. Females in such a family depend on their parents for their lives. As I was working for my education, so were they working for their dowry, the means to leave my father's control and start their own family. So, it is no mystery they aligned with his wishes. If the father said "jump," they jumped. And, of course, they would agree that I could not go to university because the family had to save money for their dowries.

It is understandable why my sisters showed me no support. Yet, it is hard to rationalize why they, too, pounced on me collectively on that fateful day, hitting me with wanton cruelty.

And I got no support from my brother. He did not like that our customers openly preferred me to him because I would go the extra mile for them. Some even came to my father and told him they supported our grocery store thanks to me! And it must have bothered my brother that moving ahead with my education meant he was getting left behind. Count my brother in my father's camp for these and other reasons.

To this day, I cannot figure out my mother. She is an enigma. Why did she have to be so cruel? Where was her basic humanity? How could she treat her own child this way? I cannot see myself doing that to a stranger. Had the war years distorted people's basic decency to such an extent? Had my father's cruelty to her warped her humane orientation? While we readily agree that wars affect people's behavior, experience shows that people can be cruel to each other, even to their own kin, at any time, warfare or not.

What could it have taken for my mother to allow me to gather some clothes, give me a few drachmas, and pack me a piece of bread? She knew I had been prevented from eating that day. She knew *I had nowhere to go*. Where was her maternal heart? Did she have any? Had anger erased all sanity and good judgment?

The day of my banning from the paternal home must have been the most important day of my life up to that point.

Do you remember when yours was?

I was reprogrammed and rebooted that day. I was transformed and metamorphosed. The old me was excised, decimated, and expunged. If there ever had been a clear dividing line in my life up to that point, it was that notorious day. If there ever was a day to leave all and never look back, that was the day.

But how could I move forward?

DEMETRIUS KOUBOURLIS PHD

6. Homeless

*O*n *my own*

I spent the night in the small room I rented at first glance in Patras, trying to collect my thoughts. As soon as it was practical, I got up the following day after a virtually sleepless night and went to see my friend, George Koufakis.

For some reason, George and I had formed a friendship from the start of our Commercial School days. His working-class parents ran a milk and yogurt delivery business, and George helped with the store as most children were expected to do. We were drawn to each other in an interesting relationship. George proved to be a devoted friend; I knew he admired me for some reason and aligned himself with me in a unique way. He would often visit me in Rion, and we occasionally did our school assignments together. Other classmates would, at times, also come to Rion to do their assignments with me.

I shared with him the news of my expulsion from the paternal home. George had more than enough empathy. We discussed what could be done. Finding a job was difficult, but I had to keep trying. Still no job after a few days.

The landlady asked for her money. She was understanding. She even gave me something to eat, but she could not wait any longer. Others wanted the room; they had cash. I was out.

Homeless, homeless, homeless! I had lost it all; my edifice had crumbled, and I was past bargaining with myself about bits of my fate. I immersed myself in my calamity wholesale. Selectivity disappeared as I went into survival mode.

Calamities cultivate stoicism.

∞∞∞∞

Psila Alonia is a square on a higher plateau in Patras. It is steeped in history and is where a brave monk declared Greek Independence from Turkey in 1821 – his statue dominates the square. It is also where the Germans hanged a dozen resistance fighters in 1943. There is even a glassed-over area where one can look at a lower level in the excavated ground -- a previous era of pre-Christian marble fragments. In addition to contemporary benches, ancient Greek marble rocks are strewn about the square and can be used to sit on. Several cafes are on the periphery.

In the fall of 1957, when I found myself on the streets, I spent about three months, most of the daytime, sitting at one of the café tables on Psila Alonia Square. As I had no money, I never bought a single drink. The waiters got used to seeing me day in and day out and let me be, as the chairs were mostly empty with the fall turning into winter. I would hold a small book on the table and support my head with a hand on each side of my face, catching some sleep while pretending to read.

I had to sleep somewhere.

And there was access to a public restroom, thank God!

Maid to the rescue

The reader surely remembers my brief relationship with Olympia, the housemaid, from my last days in Rion. By this time, her bosses had left Rion and were living in their permanent residence in Patras. As I was supposed to be studying in Italy and our educational and economic levels were disparate, our relationship had been shelved for good. However, necessity brought her back into my life's central focus. This is where our relationship changed dramatically. I managed to contact her with some difficulty -- there were no cell phones then.

As a live-in maid, Olympia had been assigned a room adjacent to the kitchen and above the stairs on one side of the house. Her masters occupied the upstairs central part of the large apartment on the other side. There was an indoor stairway leading upstairs from the main street entry. We devised a plan: she would leave the front door unlocked at night and place a plate of food under the stairs for me. It was agreed I should come every evening at midnight. After eating while sitting at the bottom step, I would go upstairs, join her in bed until 5 a.m., and leave promptly before her boss showed up for breakfast at about 6.

Putting Olympia's self-interest and motives aside, I am grateful to her for her help at this critical moment in my life.

Maid pregnant

Our routine worked as well as expected until Olympia announced she was pregnant. Without absolving myself entirely, I hold my father indirectly responsible for this. Had he kept his promises to me, I would be in Italy studying. This pregnancy seemed to seal my fate and rob whatever was left of my future. It was like the final colossal nail in my coffin.

Olympia and I agreed her pregnancy should be interrupted. My resourceful friend George asked around. One of his customers, an accountant, knew a pharmacist who could prepare an abortion pill, I was informed. We managed to obtain the funds for the tablet with considerable difficulty. I delivered it to Olympia with the appropriate instructions, secured her promise, and thought the matter was settled.

However, one must never count their chickens before they are hatched or ignore the possibility of a lurking *deus ex machina.*

Some weeks passed with Olympia vouching she had taken the abortive drug, but the pregnancy was progressing at full steam. The pill had failed, she announced. Clouds of heavier fear began descending upon me, hounding me to the ground. I conferred with George and other friends I had made at Psila Alonia. An urgent intervention was needed. One of them knew a nurse who worked for a doctor who might do an abortion. Abortions were illegal in Greece at that time. The doctor acquiesced but wanted a sum commensurate with the risk. My friends volunteered to chip in what they had; one even offered his watch. My brother, with whom I could still communicate, agreed to help but did not come through. Still, we did not have enough. Another chat followed with the nurse friend, and the doctor decided to do it for much less.

The appointed day came. The operation was a clandestine event slated for eight o'clock one evening. I took Olympia on my bike to the doctor's office, but on arrival, I was informed there would be no abortion. Was there some *deus ex machina* again that spooked the doctor?

Why did the doctor renege at the last minute?

Caught in bed

A few days went by. Early one morning, Olympia's boss unexpectedly came to wake her up at about five a.m. and caught us in bed. I immediately got up, crouching in front of him, he a bespectacled lanky six-footer, me a frightened mere 5-foot 4-inches desperately trying to keep the sheet around my naked body. He looked at me as if thinking about his next move. He brushed his right palm against my left cheek with surgical precision as if to slap me. It did not feel like a slap; it was more like a rough caress. This was not what one might have expected under the circumstances. The Greeks I knew, would not have acted in this sort of civilized way.

"Let's hope she's not pregnant," he said, meaningfully looking at Olympia and then at me.

My peripheral vision caught Olympia rushing to busy herself with the morning's kitchen chores. Olympia's boss wasted no time making his categorical pronouncement:

"Look here, if she is pregnant, you must marry her. Otherwise, you will be in serious trouble."

Olympia's family came from a mountainous village in North Central Greece with notions of strict family honor. He elaborated that several relatives lived in Patras, and two were on the police force. The intended message was that they would not hesitate to take me out if I did not marry her. He left no doubt that my very life was in danger.

Interestingly, Olympia's two policemen- relatives showed up after a short while as if from nowhere.

Had I been set up?

They took turns putting me through the threatening and intimidating wringer, seemingly performing what they considered their tradition-prescribed duty. There is no doubt that their professional experience also proved handy.

"We will get you no matter where you go. You've got to marry Olympia if you want to live!"

Olympia was now a liability for them, as close relatives were duty-bound to act decisively and use whatever means, including murder, to defend their family honor. In my case, I had no idea whether they were bluffing, but they never let that spectrum leave our discussions. What is sure is that the incident was a golden opportunity for them all, the boss and the relatives, to solve *their* problem: marrying Olympia off without a dowry!

It began to look like I was getting hoodwinked.

Imagine yourself being a lone teenager with the deck stacked entirely against you. I had an innate aversion to such tactics as I thought and acted like an idealistic young man of a noble spirit and just disposition. I felt highly distanced from such people and would rather have nothing to do with their ilk. My nature preferred civilized, logical persuasion and abhorred heavy-handed tactics.

Olympia had now become a liability for me, too.

"How old are you?" asked one of the policeman uncles, pushing the right side of his jacket aside enough for his holstered weapon to show.

"Nineteen," I said matter-of-factly.

"Hmm! You'll need to secure your parents' permission to marry because you're younger than 21."

"Get your father's OK, or you'll be in grave trouble," Olympia's other policeman relative interjected, sticking his finger in my face.

Petrified confusion had settled on my bewildered existence. Was I frightened? Had indifference permeated my tormented soul? Had apathy replaced my ambition? My life did not matter to me anymore. My life was rapidly going downhill.

∞∞∞

Fewer events can change one's life more radically than an unplanned and unwanted out-of-wedlock pregnancy. If things were complicated for me before, they had now gotten considerably worse. This single event derailed me further; getting an education now was no longer a dream but a pipe dream. If there was a way to worsen my miserable situation, I had discovered it.

Could I have escaped that mess by leaving town and trying my luck elsewhere? Of course. Could I have gone back to my parents? There is a good chance they would have taken me in on their terms and would have done their best to salvage *their* "honor." I could have even leveraged this event with them to leave Greece and study in Italy. But such thoughts never entered my mind, probably because my parental relationship had ceased to exist.

I was without a family; I was on my own.

I brushed aside prevailing social notions about Olympia's lack of education, her servant's status, and her suitability as wife material for me because I was of a different mold. I even glossed over the apparent likelihood they were lassoing me in to circumvent the dowry issue. To whoever would listen, I declared that marrying Olympia was the only honorable thing under the circumstances. And self-assuredly, I would add the rhetorical question:

"How would I want my sister to be treated in such a case?"

There was something naïve and selfless -- a tinge of altruism and idealism blended into my character. My sense of fairness trumped my self-interest. My understanding of honor likely resulted from being a community member of that environment, including family, society, religion, and church, and my undeniable naiveté may have been motivated by a strong desire to conform. I have always wanted to be thought of as a good person. Who has not?

∞∞∞∞

Have you noticed how, sometimes, when you find yourself in a bad situation, things happen to make it worse? And when you think they cannot get worse, they do? Yet, believing there is an end to a downturn and working hard to reverse it works if you have what it takes and some luck.

When does one give up?

When you give up, it depends on who you are: your make-up, your sense of self-worth, your goal, and how tenacious you can be. This is not an exhaustive list. However, if you ask me which item is the most critical, I might surprise you by choosing "self-worth."

Can you have a serious, responsible, binding conversation with yourself? Can you visualize having a face-to-face dialog with youself? Do you have enough respect for yourself (=self-esteem) to enter a binding accord? Can you push excuses aside, trample on laziness, and move ahead with your goal no matter the obstacles? Have you learned that achieving anything worthwhile means occasionally stumbling along the way? Have you learned to pick yourself up, dust yourself off, and move on unperturbed?

Shotgun wedding

It did not take me very long to figure out how to get my parents' permission to marry. But it involved deceiving them, which I had never done before. But I was able to rationalize quickly. They had deceived me twice by breaking their promises to help me study in Italy. Hence, I could do likewise, I reasoned. Besides, I believed I was in a life-or-death situation and had little choice.

I contacted my brother and explained I had an opportunity to emigrate to America. As I was planning to jump ship at some American port, I would be deported if caught. The only way to prevent that would be to marry a citizen of that country. For that, I needed to secure our father's permission as I was not of age.

The bad thing was that the scheme involved using my brother, as I was not on talking terms with my father. By necessity, my brother was deceived as well. (Sorry about that, brother!)

Sometimes, the end does justify the means.

My brother delivered my father's signed permission for me to marry without delay. If I were to attempt to explain why my father signed it, I would say he saw a benefit in it. There was a well-established tradition of immigrants sending money back home. He may have hoped this would also occur with me; besides, he had nothing to lose and would rid himself of a nuisance.

∞∞∞∞

With the age factor out of the way, the "shotgun" wedding went into high gear. Olympia's relatives were brought into the picture, and with her boss's wife, they planned a wedding ceremony for the next day, December 28, 1957. Evidently wishing to ensure things would go as planned, one of the policemen uncles insisted that Olympia and I stay at his apartment the night before the wedding. A precautionary house arrest, I suppose.

"You can sleep together tonight, but don't do anything." He admonished us using his official police manner. The narrow bed in the corridor did not prevent sleep with activity that night.

The wedding was to take place the next day, on a Saturday. Olympia's old father came from his mountain village to "give his daughter away." It became immediately apparent that I did not have proper clothing. So, early that day, he and I went shopping. We had a couple of obstacles to overcome. There was very little time before the obligatory church ceremony that morning. As there was no time for alterations, it proved difficult to find fitting clothes. So, we canvased one store after another. I would rush faster ahead of the old man to save time. I sensed he must have been worried that I might escape and did his best to keep pace with me.

We finally settled on a decent-looking outfit: a greenish coat with a squarish pattern and a matching pair of pants. Both were a bit too big for me. I did my best to camouflage the ill-fitting. The ceremony took place as planned in the famed St. Andreas church, the patron of Patras. The boss' wife had invited a few of her friends to participate.

Several of Olympia's relatives were present, but no one from my relatives showed up, as my parents were unaware of this "special" hush-hush event. There was no reception.

Peachy new life

After the wedding ceremony, Olympia's boss gave her a small sum and told us it was time to find our own place. While helping Olympia collect her few things from her room, some inexorable force led me to run my hand over the top of her armoire to ensure nothing was left behind. The top was higher than I could reach without raising my body on my toes and stretching. There, I found the abortion pill my friends and I had labored so hard to obtain. It was still unopened in the original wrapping!

Is everyone out to deceive me?

Olympia had deceived me; she had not taken the drug that had required so much effort and expense -- not a good harbinger of a marriage. Thoughts occurred to me about having been regally hoodwinked. My mind ran through the sequence of events: the timing of the boss' appearance in the bedroom, the prompt arrival of Olympia's policemen squad, the non-use of the abortion pill, and the cancellation of the scheduled abortion.

For evident and non-evident reasons, I was a good catch for Olympia and a convenient solution for her boss and relatives. The wedding was a done deal. It was too late now. I did not say anything, but I vowed not to forget. I put the unused pill in my pocket, hoping to at least return it and recoup some money.

What else could I do?

∞∞∞∞

We found a room at the house belonging to an acquaintance of Olympia's family. He was a policeman. A couple days after we moved in, the man accused Olympia of "stealing" some of his salt! In my presence, he slapped her hard on the face and abused her verbally.

He was much bigger than I was. What could I do? My best available wisdom told me to get out of there urgently. After leaving some drachmas on the mantlepiece where the salt was and forsaking our small deposit, we went to our room and packed our things –a small bundle; we had no suitcases or baggage. We put the package on my bicycle's back seat and walked off with the bike between us, not saying a word to the abusive landlord and not knowing where we would spend the night.

∞∞∞∞

I found my good friend George and shared my new grief. Wasting no time, George thought he had a solution but needed to talk to his father first. He returned immediately with "great news": his family was building a house in Psarofai, a Patras suburb on the south side of Patras. The "plaka," the first cement floor, had been laid on the foundation. Underneath, on one side, away from the street, was a basement-like opening without a door or windows. A 5 x 10 ft. space. No windows, dirt floor, barely head-standing height. We could stay there, he informed us. I named the place "the hole," as this was the most descriptive term I could find, implying no disdain or ingratitude.

My holy home

It was better than nothing, humid, to be sure, but it did not matter. It was a roof over our heads, and it was for free. Without wasting any time, I went to work cutting some reeds that were growing wild in the vicinity. I made a bed and a table, tying the reeds close together. Olympia wiped the floor with a rag – we had no broom – and we made it work as best as we could. I remember, more than once, I would wake up at night and wipe off the snails crawling on my face!

My friend George, forever caring, came to the "hole" one day, *walking* a discarded wooden door placed flat on the bicycle's seat and handlebars. That must have been a considerable distance on foot! He thought that would be better for Olympia and me than the reed bed.

What a great friend George was!

We were able to buy a few basics. Olympia had long experience with cooking and was quite ingenious. While the dowry cash lasted, we had some bread, potatoes, and olive oil. Later, we were reduced to eating the bark of trees and even grass. How can I forget how hungry I was? The thought has often crossed my mind that my growth was probably stunted at this time due to malnutrition.

Life was toughening me up, though. While events tormented my not-yet-mature body, they must have also tested and steeled my spirit. Most importantly, I was recuperating some of my ambition. I had to get out of that misery, or else. There was no thought about suicide at this time. Not this boy! I was going to find a way out -- I promised myself repeatedly. I vowed, I guaranteed, and made my irreversible pact with myself.

Yet, I needed to put food on our reed table without delay. I had to have a job. My tutoring was not generating much cash.

∞∞∞∞

I got a job at one of the downtown hotels with floor cleaning and reception duties. Right away, my English and Italian got noticed in the land of ignorance – the hotel owner even proposed I manage his future hotel in Corfu, an island some distance from Patras. As the Sixth Fleet had anchored in Patras, a co-worker and I accepted the hotel owner's suggestion to open a bar for American sailors. We chipped in 150 drachmas each and rented the space next to the hotel where my job was. My brother painted an "American Bar" sign on a piece of cardboard, which we hung over the entrance. We saw a steady stream of sailors eagerly buying our reasonably priced, high-quality Greek wines.

After my friend George visited me at the "bar" one day, my partner accused me of drinking the business wine with my friends. The accusation was too much for my pride as I was a total teetotaler.

I got indignant and told my partner he could keep my down payment and all else – I did not want to have anything to do with him. The hotel owner tried to make peace. I was uncompromising. He told me he would hold my share of the money to claim whenever I felt like it. I never asked for it, although I desperately needed it for survival. It is this "stupid" attitude that I call pride. The same trait would not permit me to "go back crawling" to my father's home, and it would surface in my life repeatedly.

(About thirty years later, I went to Patras and stayed at the same hotel. I saw the owner, an affable old man by then. Of course, he didn't remember me, and I said nothing about my compounded-interest-Greek fortune, which he had presumably been holding for me all those years. Far from being the end of the story, this incident, right or wrong, gave rise to one of my "business principles." I determined never to have a partner again. And I've stuck to it. Lucrative deals requiring partners presented themselves, but I kept returning to that bitter lesson and went through life solo, bypassing tempting opportunities.

I can't say I regret it.)

∞∞∞∞

After my parents learned about my shotgun wedding, I received vile letters from my brother and father, which I still have. My father threatened to kill me if I stepped into his house. My brother warned me against doing so because Father meant it.

My father had a well-developed vocabulary of insults, which he used liberally and frequently. He would use the appropriate intonation and a loud voice to ensure everyone, including the neighbors, heard him. It made me feel awful and ashamed. I would go away if it were not during mealtimes.

I dreamed of a life of mutual respect. My father taught me how not to behave through his uncivil conduct. In a twisted way, I am grateful to him for that.

"You come to the 'koryto' (the feeding trough)," he would utter with a gotcha expression when we came around to have our meals. We felt grateful if that was all, not the prelude for much more. It is a miracle that the family members' sense of self-esteem was as good as it was, given so much verbal abuse. It is reasonable to suppose that the high occurrence of insults diluted their effectiveness. We considered ourselves fortunate if his attacks remained only verbal; physical abuse sporadically accompanied his verbal abuse.

Some people enjoy singing and playing an instrument. My father may have found some sadistic enjoyment in occasionally beating my brother, me, and even my mother as if we were his instrument. In "The Beating," one of my stories included in *Sometimes Cruel* (Axios Eclectics, 2023), I describe how I ended his physical abuse of me by using an effective defense, which would elicit complaints from him even years later during my visits to Greece. He clearly saw my self-defense as a complete disregard for his parental right to physically abuse his family.

Family remembers

One day, unexpectedly, my brother paid me a visit while pregnant Olympia and I were starving in the Psarofai "hole." He was dressed in very fashionable, flashy clothing. He donned an expensive pair of dark glasses, motorcycle gloves, and a showy new belt. He was also riding what must have been a new moped. I presumed he had found out my whereabouts from my friend George.

He brought me nothing. NOTHING!

Why did he come? Had he missed me? I do not think so. It is very likely he came to show off his material possessions or that my mother had asked him to find out how I was doing. Whatever. He came empty-handed. He saw where I lived and how I lived. He never came back. Yet, years later, he would complain that I did not help him remodel the hotel my father had turned over to him, even though I had done so once in 1965. I had sent money for the remodeling of the hotel so they could get their license reissued.

How can one even begin to do justice comparing my need for survival food with declining to finance the remodeling of his hotel?

People's sensitivity to the needs of others varies. We tend to have a built-in inclination to maximize our needs and minimize those of others. I am wary of making that mistake myself.

What is certain is that my condition was well-known to them. They must have discussed it. I can see my father ranting about how he was teaching that so-and-so a lesson, and sooner or later, I would beg to be admitted back into his kingdom.

But they did not know how deep my wound was! Death by starvation was not a bad alternative to living with my exploitative father again, under his aegis and control. Freedom, even cold and famished freedom, was sweeter than cruel subjugation.

∞∞∞∞

Sometime after my brother's visit, I learned that George's mother had something for me. I went to visit her. She was an unusually gentle woman and extremely kind to me. I knew instinctively she liked me a lot. She had a world of empathy for me and my plight. I went to their store; she took me to the children's bedroom. She pointed to a paper grocery bag on the foot of the bed.

"Your mother brought this for you today," she said. "She was asking about you."

I looked over the few groceries; it was a tasty selection. I had not seen anything like this in a long while; I could smell the sausages and cheese. I closed my eyes and savored their radiating delicacy. Although exceedingly tempted, I put them back.

"I don't want them," I stated categorically and definitively; I started to leave. George's mother could not believe it; she knew Olympia and I were starving. She had given us a cup of unsold yogurt a couple of times. I thanked her and went back to my voluntary starvation.

Who needs victuals when one has a belly full of pride?

Was it pride or anger? Profound, indelible anger?

How could I accept anything from you when you tossed me out so heartlessly and unjustly? Can you wash off your guilt and atone for this incredible injury with a bag of groceries? I don't need you. I am going to make it on my own.

Even nowadays, as I write this, tears come to my eyes. Chances are you think it was foolish of me to act this way. I have done likewise on other occasions later in my life. Irrational or otherwise, this is a definite character trait of mine; I can do no more than acknowledge it. It is what it is.

A child is born

The winter was still in full gear. My good friend George would visit us regularly. It felt good seeing him and experiencing his friendship. All was not lost. There was still one solid link with empathetic humanity. He did not fail to notice how the cold was affecting pregnant Olympia. One day, he came back with great news. He had persuaded his father to let us use the shed, a structure not larger than 10 ft. by 10 ft., which was not far from our "hole," about a couple hundred yards away. It had a door and a window. I imagined some previous owner had built it as a temporary residence while constructing the dream house closer to the road. I had wondered more than once why we had not been allowed to use it instead of the hole in the first place. But life has taught me to be grateful while at the same time controlling my greed.

Without wasting a minute, we moved our possessions into the shed. This must have been one of my quickest moves to a new dwelling, as all we had could be wrapped in a single bundle. Of course, I also moved the door bed and the reed table in minutes.

My first-born

We still lived in the shed on June 15, 1958, when Olympia gave birth to a healthy girl without complications. I remember picking her up from the Patras General Hospital. I doubt that I got excited like brand-new fathers are supposed to be. It was another unplanned event in my drifting life. Subconsciously, anything that took me away from education was nothing to cheer about. Nevertheless, I grew to make the child part of my life and to love her very much.

Wife's dowry

As I understood the custom in Greece those days, better-to-do families would take in an underage female child from a poor family as a servant. There was no salary, just room and board, but with the understanding that marrying off was part of the deal as the dowry custom placed an unbearable burden on poor families.

In that context, I got the idea that Olympia's boss was getting away with a lot. He paid for the wedding ceremony and gave Olympia a tiny amount, barely enough to live modestly for a month or two. I weighed this in my mind and pressed Olympia to approach her matron with a request.

This was when my tutoring, however minor, was putting some food on the table. I was no longer working at the downtown hotel. I would ride my bicycle to the students' homes to deliver the lesson. As distances varied and were sometimes considerable, I invested much time between classes. I thought a moped would serve well. It did not have to be new, only in good condition. I reasoned that with a moped, I could cover greater distances, teach more students, and earn more income without exhausting myself.

At first, Olympia thought it was a bad idea. But I managed to persuade her, and she presented the request. I am not privy to how her former boss understood the in-house servitude custom, his agreement with her parents, and whether he had something to hide. But after a brief hesitation, he agreed, and I got myself my motor-powered wheels. However minor, this was Olympia's dowry, a must for any bride in the Greece of my time.

B.P.
Big Poverty, Big Plans

∞∞∞∞

To cure a disease, it helps to know what the disease is. My disease was poverty. No, Big Poverty. That would be my label, the definition of the malady afflicting me.

I cut a small rectangular piece of cardboard and carefully wrote BP on it -- nothing else. My six years of calligraphy came in handy. I punched two holes on one side with a pointed knife and stuck the license-like sign on the back of the moped. This was going to be my license plate, only it did not identify the moped – it identified my station in life, Big Poverty.

With the moped in my possession, I put my plan into practice. The number of students increased, and we could move to a real house. We found a one-bedroom rental in Psarofai, the suburb where our "hole" was. We were no longer starving.

Zero social net

Before I leave this account of my troubled life, examining the community's role in helping others seems appropriate. I knew nobody to turn to for help, food, or shelter. The community I grew up and lived in was more intent on keeping its members under a scrutinizing eye of religious and social conformity. It had no social net that I knew or took advantage of.

As for assistance from relatives, there was absolutely none for me. A case in point: During my peregrinations for subscribers to the Magazine for the Blind after I had left the parental house for the first time, I once went door-to-door through a village near Patras. One of my uncles, Vasilios, ran a butcher shop there. It was late in the day; the evening lights were turned on, and my uncle's butcher shop was open. We immediately noticed each other as I approached and as he came around a hanging sheep carcass. He showed mild surprise but not particular pleasure to see me. I explained my "mission" and invited him to subscribe, which he did for the minimum period. After thanking him, I asked about a hotel for the night, hoping he would offer a spot in his house. He obliged by giving me the hotel information, but he did not offer me his hospitality! He was my uncle, my mother's elder brother.

Years later, when I was successful and prosperous, he would go out of his way to connect with me during my visits to Greece. He would ingratiate himself, repeatedly apologizing for not taking me in that night. He even invited my family and me to lunch in his modest home when we visited Greece. When my mother died, he undertook to console my brother and me with some ouzo and a special meat delicacy he had been saving for a special occasion – bull's testicles!

Why are people sometimes anxious to help others when it is unnecessary but do not do so when needed? Why are they eager to assist you when you have money but turn the other way when you do not?

Furthermore, Uncle Vasilios showed tremendous pride in being related to me. On one of my trips to Greece, I took a copy of a book containing pictures and biographical information about distinguished Greeks abroad. I was included in this book. Uncle Vasilios "borrowed" that copy from my father and would not return it despite persistent requests. He would go to the local cafes eager to show the book to his friends and whoever would listen, luxuriating in his relation to me.

Another brother of my mother's, Elias, had a lovely house in a good neighborhood near the outskirts of Patras. He was the one who had loaned me his mandolin but who expected to be paid for it. He also "loaned" me a bible, which, in time, he retrieved. During my ban time from the parental home, I was recruited to tutor his two sons in English. I went to their house repeatedly, quite a distance. They never paid or fed me, although I could have used some of both.

Once my marriage to Olympia became known, I met Uncle Elias on the road to Patras. I had just finished tutoring his sons and left his house. He was walking across from me on the main road, going in the opposite direction. I called out to him repeatedly, and he gave me the cold shoulder – he must have disapproved of my recent shotgun marriage.

While he was negligent in paying for my tutoring or assisting me in my hour of need, he was unfailing in ostracizing me for my shotgun marriage. Tradition trumps decency. Quick social condemnation, but debt noncompliance.

In fact, I received no help from any of my relatives during my time of need. However, some were later quick to expect and sometimes demand that I share my good fortune with them; mind you, whatever wealth transfer they expected from me was not for their survival but rather to boost their financial fortune at my expense. They would often hint at my lack of generosity to them by relating accounts of other emigrated Greeks who had given much or much more money to their relatives. I learned to let such comments in one ear and out the other, but it was a frequent litany that I had to endure. In my mind, there was an endless refrain playing:

"Where were you when I was dying of hunger?"

7. Dr. Carleton French

The Power returns

I am 19 years old. I am an English language tutor. I am walking along Korinthos Street in Patras, Greece. I have just finished one private lesson and am free for the next two hours. It is about 11 am.

The sidewalks were under roof cover on this venerable street. The worn stone pavement bore proof of multigenerational foot traffic. Gratitude belongs to lives long gone for creating this grand sidewalk. Stores and dwelling entrances were packed next to each other – no unused space -- evidencing a prized real estate past.

The doors were a lot taller than modern doors.

One entry, wooden and clearly very old, is now immediately to my right. It has two leaves. The door's right leaf is open. A tripod sign in front of the door's left leaf reads: "Greek-American Cultural Institute Now Open. Come In." I glance to my right. A flight of stairs with well-worn stone steps leads somewhere upstairs.

It is lit with whatever natural light can get through. As I climb to the first landing, a closed door fills my view: "Director's Office."

The door is closed. To my left, the stairs continue. A wave of energetic students is spilling down the stairs. They make room for me to continue my way upstairs.

I reach the top of the stairs. A large, poorly lit corridor opens to my left and right. It is empty. All the doors are closed except for one.

The late morning sunlight flooding the room, a classroom, sharply silhouettes a tallish figure standing behind an ordinary classroom desk, stacking students' assignments together. The glass-rimmed profile of a handsome man is focused on the collected papers. The vivid sunlight pierces the man's slightly curled locks of hair on the top of his head. He is fair-skinned. He could be north-European, not Greek. An off-color short-sleeve shirt and generic pants offer no clue about the man's provenience.

My view takes in the rest of the room. It is an empty classroom. Several long, narrow top desks, each with rows of chairs behind them, populate the space. Four tall, thin, old-fashioned, single-pane windows dominate the wall facing me, paralleling the busy street below.

I do not quite know what I am doing here. It is as if some power directed my steps to this spot precisely at this moment: the class has just concluded, all the students are gone, and I am standing in front of the only open door on the second floor, facing the teacher as he is about to leave.

Perfect timing! For what? What am I doing here, really? Why am I here? Did someone or something orchestrate this? Am I being guided?

I am standing in the corridor at the threshold of the open door, hypnotized, devoid of purpose or initiative.

Becoming aware of my presence, the man turns his bespectacled face toward me, drawing a welcoming smile as if towards an expected guest. I smile back.

I always like to smile. Smiling is an amicable weapon, little used in Greece at that time. Smile at your own peril. You smile, and you raise suspicions. If you are a female minding your own business, my best advice is to avoid smiling at the opposite sex altogether.

"Good morning!" he utters in English, and I respond likewise. "Are you looking to join us?" he asks with a distinctive American accent.

"Not exactly," I respond with my best English pronunciation. The man turns towards me, his whole-body language expressing polite interest.

"Oh, you speak English! Come in!" Still zombie-like, but without hesitation, I cross the threshold. I stretch out my right hand. Our hands connect in a warm welcome.

"My name is Jim," I introduce myself, using the version of my name employed in Greece.

"I am Dr. Carlton French," he responds. He wants to know where I learned my English; he compliments me and shows interest in discovering how deep my language knowledge goes. He puts his papers in a folder and into a black briefcase. "I was about to leave; I am done for the day," he says. "Perhaps we can walk out together," he continues.

"Sure, with pleasure," I respond, only too happy to have such a golden opportunity to practice my English.

At this time, in 1958, only scant occasions presented themselves for English language practice. The renowned American 6th Fleet, roaming the Mediterranean, visited our waters occasionally, offering rare contact opportunities. Really, meeting this American in Patras at this time was a godsend.

We walk toward the exit. Dr. French locks the door, and we slowly walk down the stairs as our conversation continues. He resumes his compliments on my English language proficiency, showing genuine amazement. He also volunteers that I speak better than the Greek director of the Institute in Athens. I find it hard to imagine, and I cannot help but feel elated. Is he really exaggerating, I wonder?

I learned my English at the Patras Emporiki Sxoli (Commercial School), where I made my teacher proud, I have been told. I attended some classes at an English language institute, where the teacher loaned me a textbook and let me participate for free in a few lessons. I worked on my own all I could by reading just about every English language book available at the small Patras American Information Service Library. I also aced the Michigan University English Language Certificate exam. I would like to think my English, whatever its level, was higher than what Dr. French had been exposed to in Greece, and that is good enough for an explanation for all practical purposes.

Leaving the closed classroom door, we amble down the stairs and the sidewalk. The springtime sun is bright but not hot. Soon, we reach King George Square, the central square in Patras. Suddenly, Dr. French turns to me, looking me straight in the eyes. As if making an official announcement, he utters these unforgettable words:
"I'll put you on the map." I had never heard the expression before and tried to guess what he meant. I thought I had understood his metaphor. Turning toward me, he puts his right arm on my left shoulder and asks: "How would you like to become my assistant at the Institute?" Wow!!! What??? Had I heard right? Had I understood correctly?
Seeing how dumb-founded I am, he proceeds to explain. He proposes that I teach the Institute's two lower English language classes while he continues leading the two advanced ones. Now I

understand good and well and cannot believe my good fortune. A vast door is opening in front of me and for me alone. This is not a dream come true, as there has not been such a dream in my consciousness. This is mana from heaven.

Bright, new horizon

The outcome of running into this outstanding person gave birth to a psychological buoyancy I had not felt in my strenuous existence up to this time. It was a high such as I had never experienced before. I had lived with one big dream for as long as I could remember. And yes, I had a vision of a better life. I wanted to leave Greece. Do not ask me why it is so or whether I hated Greece. I am not xenophilic, either. One can even boldly suppose that just about any ambitious young Greek wanted badly to emigrate. Somehow, the idea had long been entrenched that one could not make it in Greece but could do so in some foreign country. Over decades, Greeks, by the thousands, have emigrated to America, Australia, and other countries. My maternal grandfather and his two brothers worked on the California railroad in the early twentieth century.

∞∞∞∞

My tutoring load increased dramatically thanks to my affiliation with the Greek-American Cultural Institute. I could stack one teaching session after another and leverage the physical distance with my moped. However, the obvious occurred to me as my time became scarcer. Why not have group tutoring? The cost to the student would be reduced, and the benefit to the teacher would be increased – a win-win situation.

It was more practical to leave our suburb residence in Psarofai and move to Patras, where the student market was. I found a two-bedroom house facing a sizeable square. One room became our bedroom, and the other the classroom. A blackboard was attached to one of the walls, and several seats were procured – an adequate classroom. I was exceedingly busy teaching at the Institute, at home, and giving private lessons. It was tiring, and I remember falling asleep once during a private class.

∞∞∞∞

Sometime later, Dr. French floated the idea of establishing a Greek-American Institute extension class in Rion, where my father's home was. Until then, there had been no contact with my parents since they had banned me. Dr. French encouraged me to reconnect with them, and a visit was arranged. We had lunch with my parents at Father's house while I served as the interpreter.

My old elementary school teacher, who still lived in Rion, heard of the idea of an English class and approached me with good news -- he had procured a room to be used as a classroom for free! For some reason, nothing came of the plan to establish an English class in Rion, probably because Dr. French left Greece shortly afterward or I had no time.

∞∞∞∞

Dr. French was a cultivated person. His French was impeccable, and his piano playing was impressive. All this complimented his patrician appearance to a tee. He had also done missionary work. I was exceedingly impressed with him and felt proud to be his Greek liaison; he called me "my son." He was slim, as were most people in their fifties those years, and he moved with ease and natural grace. And unlike most everyone those days, he did not smoke.

More than once, I witnessed his humility and eagerness to admit error. All my experience up to that point was of the absolute kind: it went something like this: intelligent people do not make mistakes, and if they do, they never admit it. It is black and white, with zero relativism. Education and culture have something to do with it. Uneducated or poorly educated people are afraid to admit error, guarding their meager intellectual storehouse with zeal, possibly due to a lack of intellectual ammunition to defend their views.

Baptismal branding

Children in Greece are not given a name upon birth. The time came to baptize my child, as was the strict custom. Dr. French felt flattered when I asked him to be the godfather. Three names were chosen: Carletona, Sophia, and Margarita. His choice was first and third, and the middle was mine. As the child was a female, my mother's name, Sophia, would be a canonical choice. Naming a boy after one's father and a girl after one's mother was an inviolate custom, more or less; it was the traditional way to show respect for your parents. I remember the baptism very well. It felt as if something was happening to me, but I was not a part of it.

Custom and law required that the child's name be officially registered. I went to the proper authorities, anticipating a routine event. Instead, I was confronted with an unshakable bureaucracy.

"There is no saint by such a name. "Carletona" is no saint's name!" I was told. "This name cannot be registered."

The result can be unpredictable when narrow-mindedness gets a hold of society. But when organized ignorance becomes ritualized, be prepared for a bigger surprise. This was another reason for me not wanting to be part of such a society.

But "Sophia" was an acceptable name as there was a saint by that name -- it was stated. And so it came to pass that Carletona was named Sophia, but it did not prevent us from calling the child by our chosen name.

The servant of God, ~~Carletona~~ Sophia ~~Margarita~~, is baptized in the name of the Father. Amen. And the Son. Amen. And...

A SACRED RITUAL FOR THE LITTLE ONE

America, open thy doors!

I repeatedly shared with Dr. French my desire to obtain a higher education. How great it would be if I could attend an American University! He explained the simple application procedure for admission to one's chosen university. There was no need to have political clout or family riches or to endure a whimsical entrance exam. One could even apply to more than one university at the same time!

What could be more straightforward than that?

This is the fabulous secret my "educated" and uneducated circles did not know or kept away from me! Lest the reader fail to comprehend this significant difference, I feel urged to juxtapose the Greek and the American approaches to education confronting me at the time. The former was focused on keeping the citizens in perpetual darkness; the latter encouraged an educated citizenry. Don't you see why I wanted no part of the one and all I could get of the other? America was the natural country for me; Greece of that time was not. I was fashioned for America; I belonged in America. Greece was an accident; America was my choice!

Aside from its economic advantages, America impressed me as a place with a radically different attitude. The system existed for the benefit of all, not the entrenched minority whose goal was to creatively throw as many obstacles in your way as possible. In the United States, all sorts of endless opportunities, colleges, universities, and vocational schools welcomed everyone, especially well-motivated students. One had a choice, a magnificent choice, a blessed choice. *No one could dictate you cannot have an education.* No one would compel you to wait for your sisters to get married, do military service before attending university, or work for free. No one could wave a menacing tradition as an excuse to stop you from enlightening your mind and becoming a better all-around person.

America presented me with a reasoned system; Greece threw a wall of obstructionist whimsicality at me.

I pictured America's doors open, and not only for education. If your goal was to become rich, America was beckoning. Opportunities abounded and were ripe for the picking – it was all up to you, not to any high-handed bureaucrat or self-appointed gatekeeper. You only needed to want to succeed and be ready to sweat for it. This is what I understood the American Dream to mean.

After obtaining the addresses of half a dozen California schools and Dr. French's fantastic letter of recommendation, I applied. Acceptance responses rained on me. I chose California State College in Sacramento for no reason other than it was a place in America, the home of the free!

8. Equipment for the American Dream

Self-worth
It increasingly began looking like I was really going to America. No more Greek obstacles would stand in the way. Neither society nor government, not even family, could stop me. My meeting with my American destiny was set. I would leave many negative memories behind and start a new life. And I was confident success was inevitable.

What equipment was I taking with me?

∞∞∞∞

Ambition must have been one characteristic that distinguished my brother from me. I could not wait to get going with my life -- I had an ironclad rendezvous with success. I had my star to follow and was keenly aware. It felt like a mission. I am not stating that my brother was not ambitious. He must have certainly been that in his way. However, having dreams is not the same as having burning plans. The latter comes with urgency and impatience; the former is more passive -- not all dreams come with plans.

I still have a little journal that I kept in my early teens. It contains a free-hand graph showing a timeline slowly rising and then taking off. It is a graphic, simple-minded depiction of how an ambitious

14-year-old boy visualizes his future. Far from drifting, I was urgently goal-oriented.

I often wonder what bit of difference there was in me that enabled me to withstand some heavy blows in life or to follow some directions and avoid others. Why did I go one way and my brother another, for instance? What was the attribute present in me and absent in my brother? Or, what was a characteristic in my brother but missing in me? I cannot pretend to have the best answer, but I have some ideas based on my life's events. And I cannot possibly claim to know all the obstacles my brother had to confront and how he faced them. However, I keep returning to the equipment nature grants us: some of us are strong, some are weak, some are beautiful, others are not, some have wealthy parents, some do not, some are evil, and some are not, and so forth. Like it or not, we are born unequal and are dealt a different hand going through life.

∞∞∞∞

I was filled with boundless confidence and optimism, an adamant desire for university education, and the ability and willingness to work hard.

I was also loaded with a priceless notion of *self-worth,* so necessary to achieve my full potential. This human aspect has not always received its due attention. I regard it as one of the most valuable weapons in one's arsenal. How high an opinion we hold of our intrinsic values and how much we demand of ourselves as we go through life determines our success. Confidence in ourselves, abilities, and resilience gives us the required durable resolve.

 I must assume we all desire the best for ourselves. However, it is so much easier to take it easy. Laziness and rationalization are our enemies, our nemesis; they stand in the way of genuine accomplishment. A wise approach is recognizing the enemy a priori and appropriately raising our defenses. Not everyone is able or willing to combat this enemy.

A solid sense of self-worth paired with ambition is a powerful combination. Success is guaranteed if wisdom and good luck get into the mix and are fueled by hard work.

∞∞∞∞

My father's proposal to sell chestnuts at the local ferry was as inconceivable to me as it could possibly get. In an environment of few high school graduates, I had just finished the high school equivalent, was better versed in English than my coevals, and had a fair knowledge of Italian and French, among other accomplishments. I had every reason to hold a high opinion of myself. Furthermore, I was well-read; I could write prose and poetry and even talk extemporaneously in verse. There was something on which to base my higher self-esteem. I was proud of myself. I possessed justified pride.

Sorry, Father, I could not possibly visualize myself peddling chestnuts on a ferry.

∞∞∞

My battered self-esteem had a solid sense of self-worth to lean on.

My self-worth has been my protector and motivator in the struggle for success in life. It has enabled sane risk-taking to embrace new, challenging opportunities and pursue exciting possibilities.

Growth and success without risk-taking are generally not possible. In addition, creating and sustaining new positive relationships is a straightforward consequence of success. Gaining the admiration of your cohorts provides tremendous fuel for further growth. While assertiveness in tackling life's challenges takes one outside one's comfort zone, it is the way to success and even toward a higher sense of self-worth and emotional stability.

Show me a person with low self-esteem, and I will look for waning self-worth. Success comes from within. However, opportunities emerge in our lives; someone opens doors for us, a marriage to a wealthy family, etc. What we do with those opportunities is our affair; we need good equipment to deal with luck's offerings. It does not hurt to have a sense of high self-worth in addition to whatever other attributes nature graced us with.

My sense of self-worth emerged intact despite my father's frequent verbal and physical attacks on my self-esteem. Try explaining that.

∞∞∞

I often wonder whether what distinguished me from the rest of my family might not have been what caused them to ostracize me. There came a time when they resented my being perceived as better or behaving as if I were. One can understand and even justify their resentment. You grow up just like them, in the same environment, and one day, you raise your flag of independence, acting like you are better than them. You may not state that literally, but your differentness, improved vocabulary, thoughts, and ideas may grate on the ears of your siblings and parents. "Just who do you think you are? And why do you think you're better than us?"

Putting yourself above others is not a way to make friends and influence people.

Thus, due to my feeling of high self-worth, chances are I alienated even those members of my family who might agree with me in some way. My precious self-worth fueled my progress but may also have created obstacles. Be all that as it may, I must conclude that a high feeling of self-worth is one of the best allies one can have in life. It is that steel rod holding you standing despite life's repeated blows.

Use of time

Time is our most precious commodity. Life is an arena where things happen. One's life is one's personal arena. Life is cast against the background of time. No matter what you do, day in and day out, you chip away at your allotted time. You have some control over what you do with your time. Unfortunately, most of the time, we make the wrong choices and waste this precious commodity. Lamentably, the allotted time is taken away from many others for reasons outside their control.

Most people are consumers of time. I strove to be a user of time.

I deal with time in great reverence. My happiest moments are when my time gets used wisely. I am grateful not too much time has been taken away from me, that I have had some control over my time, and that I have been given time till now. I hope there will be more time for me going forward, but I have no way of knowing. It is an assumption I must operate by; it is how it is for all of us.

Various cultures have found ways to personify and even deify time. Chronos in Greek Mythology is an example, and so is Kala in Hinduism. Time's influence over my life has left a permanent sense of hurrying, not having enough time to learn everything I want to understand, and leaving me dissatisfied. Setting psychological considerations aside, this condition does not make me unhappy. On the contrary, it is a driving force and a source of regenerative direction. Learning for me is akin to a profession, or perhaps more than a profession. Maybe it is like a boundless and passionate avocation that makes going through life such a wonderful experience.

Making money is an activity that, sooner or later, a wise mind determines to be essentially unworthy of the time invested. Making lots of money and building oneself monuments or recirculating trite ideas, like the longest yacht and the like, clearly show the limitations of the intellect or intellectual bankruptcy. Making money is a time robber. It has been so for me. Having to make money for survival is clearly justifiable and necessary. But making money to make more than you need requires additional justification.

I have not been as wise with the use of my time as I could have been. But I have not ceased to strive for a better use of my time. Greed and glory have been my enemies. I plead guilty.

I regret that the necessity to work to put myself through undergraduate school compelled me to spend less time on my education than I would have liked to. So much time working nights, trying to rush my assignments, and not devoting more or adequate time to my subjects pained me. I wanted so much to learn for the sake of learning, not just to get a degree. With time and the lack thereof, learning became somewhat secondary to piling on the necessary credits to graduate without delay. How I regret this!

In general, pursuing my education was a holy goal, a sacred task whose sanctitude was sallied by the exigencies of life. Oh, how I wish it were not so! Having to earn a living and an education were in fervent competition. Time was the bone of contention. Giving more to the one meant taking it from the other.

Why could it not have been just education? There was and is so much I have wanted to learn! This is one of my regrets. I despise people who are being offered fantastic opportunities to do university study but who opt to waste their time with alcohol and drugs. I have little tolerance for such behavior. As the expression goes, I would have given an arm and a leg to have the privileges afforded them.

Obtaining an education is one of life's worthiest goals. Right or wrong, I view it as the first obligation after survival is assured. I have in mind the kind of education that prepares minds for critical consideration of information, cultivates life-improving capabilities, and contributes to the quality of everyone's existence, creating worthy citizens. I envision education as that sacrosanct process of excising ignorance and its blind confidence. I see education as that process that scrapes away the dangers lurking in dark, unenlightened minds bent on destruction and evil. I imagine education as a magical process via which human life improves with time.

As I ponder my culture's moral hold on me, whether it originated with religion or upbringing, I celebrate my gradual selective emancipation from both. I have come to understand why, time and again, I went against my self-interest to please my father. I was up against powerful forces that had been at work long before my birth. I realized that my personal emancipation toolkit included whatever critical thinking abilities education and reflection have afforded me.

Critical thinking enables the individual to be actively aware of the difference between the socialization process and brainwashing. While the former has a neutral connotation, the latter is anything but neutral, as its coercive nature is often unethical and may even be illegal. Both socialization and brainwashing are forms of social control; they endeavor to inculcate ways of influencing norms, values, and beliefs through various means such as culture, upbringing, education, media, peer interactions, religion, and politics.

Very often, fear interferes with critical thinking. Attempts to change people's minds and behavior through stigmatization and punishment are not ingredients of a healthy society. Respecting one's rights and promoting shared values is not easy. The well-being of a society's members relies on respecting individual autonomy, allowing the freedom to question and form one's opinions, even if those opinions differ from prevailing ones. Censorship of viewpoints different from our own is not what critical thinking is all about. Agreeing to disagree is a simple dictum that carries a lot of weight.

Luck AWOL

Even though my arsenal for success may have included all the ammunition mentioned above, the presence or absence of luck, like it or not, cannot be ignored. Good luck means an opportune match between one's abilities and the opportunities presented. But no such convergence is valuable unless it is wisely taken advantage of. The Roman philosopher Seneca certainly had it right: "Luck is what happens when preparation meets opportunity."

I often mention luck as a factor in pivotal moments in one's life. As there is good and evil, black and white, etc., so is luck and lack thereof.

Luck did not favor me in the dowry matter; it was absent. I had two sisters who needed dowries – lots of money! -- to get married. The whole family was enslaved to that obligation. The sisters' dowries were the family's albatross and the death sentence to my educational dream.

Had I been born thirty years later, luck would have been on my side, as the Greek dowry system was abolished in 1983!

Luck was also dormant with Greek university availability. The irony of ironies: the University of Patras, a major university in the Balkans, was established in 1964, only a decade too late for me, *precisely in my hometown*, just a few minutes walk from where I was born, grew up, and lived!

Thus, the two major obstacles in my life vanished all by themselves when it was too late to do me any good. Luck was out of sync with my own educational needs. It was totally absent when I needed it. In fact, this is an occasion to refer to as anti-luck, not merely the absence of luck but the presence of bad luck galore.

My father might have found another reason to prevent me from continuing my education, and the military would have eaten up a couple of years. The deck was stacked against me. Many would have given up a lot sooner. But some inscrutable force, like a steel rod inside me, kept me unbendingly dedicated to my cause and calling. Some would say it was divine support, but I prefer acknowledging it without bold, inductive commentary. The perception remains that it goaded me and guided me unwaveringly. That inner force provided enormous energy and formidable tenacity to overcome all obstacles, and it may have been the good luck in my genes. It served me with consistency and constancy. For that, I acknowledge it with humility and gratitude. Put another way, luck is what we encounter in our life's journey and what life equipped us with before the journey started.

9. Readying for departure

A burden of a wife

A I must not have paid sufficient attention to Olympia, my wife, what with my back-to-back teaching load and our fundamental differences. During all our time together, she cared for the house chores and our child as best as her moods allowed her to. But I did not regard her as a partner for life. We were very different. Our conversations were limited to the quotidian and no more. It was an imbalanced relationship because of the difference in character, education, and cultural attitudes, let alone my aspirations. Unplanned and accidental circumstances had brought us together. She was on the ground; I was in the air. She was of the earth; I was of the ether, or so I thought.

Despite my gratitude for Olympia's help during my first couple of months of homelessness, I soon felt burdened by her and my obligations to our little family. I resented her deceiving me about the pregnancy and the abortion medicine; indeed, her coming into my life had complicated my already desperate situation. Although I understood that everyone has a right to a better life (not necessarily at my expense, to be sure), I felt like a victim -- I had been taken.

Was I a victim?

Was it not my choice to hook up with her in the first place and to be careless in the second? Yes, it was. We can blame nature for that. Yet none of that would have happened had my father kept his promises to support my education.

∞∞∞∞

One day, when I returned from teaching at the Greek-American Cultural Institute, I saw a commotion around the front of our home. A neighbor lady brought me up to speed. An ambulance had just taken Olympia to the hospital. As soon as I entered the house, I found a note from her, which I still have. "You are a good man. I am leaving this world. Goodbye." I rode my moped to the hospital and arrived as she was about to be released. I picked her up, and we went home. She had inflicted a tiny superficial wound on her chest on the right side close to the clavicle bone and had no trouble riding on the back seat of my moped. I said nothing until we got home safely. An angry volcano was about to burst inside me.

"Why did you do it?" I asked, holding my teeth tight, trying to contain the fuming flood inside me. I was feeling ashamed vis-à-vis the whole world out there. She would not respond, and it was not necessary anyway. It was not difficult to figure out. She had staged the entire thing, seeking attention, as one might say. Or, aiming to embarrass me, I would suggest. She promised not to do it again, and I chose to drop the matter, becoming more determined than ever that she was the wrong person in my life.

Straying Libido

As if I did not have enough problems, what with a wife and child and the oppressive ambition plaguing me, fantasizing and romanticizing also beleaguered my mind. Was it a natural escape from my troubles? Like most people, I rush to blame my libido as if nature had not given me any wisdom and I had not learned my lessons. Fortunately, I had learned some lessons and strove to keep myself in line.

If Olympia was not my chosen one and was far from my ideal woman, there had to be others out there. Enter Katerina, one of my English language students; her father was a Patras banker. I went to their house at seven p.m. three times a week to deliver my private English language lesson. She was a bright eighteen-year-old with solid romantic feelings, and I was a married twenty-year-old who should have known better. She signaled her availability and was not timid in her approach. I did not seek her sexual favors, yet I proved somewhat civilly accommodating, and a fiery correspondence ensued. Although we met three times a week in her house for our lesson, we maintained strict decorum – there was no physical contact between us.

Katerina's imagination took flight. No one in my life before or since has written such high-quality stuff dedicated to me. It struck my heart's kindling and ignited it. I often wonder what kind of inspiration our sex drive can provide and how benign we would be if it did not exist. She wrote reams and reams in transliterated Greek using the Latin alphabet to mislead the suspicious and provide some kind of cover. I still have some of her letters, salvaged after a cataclysmic event described later.

∞∞∞∞

If springtime is a great season to fall in love, summertime may be the time to go to the beach. The idea was to have a beach outing for all my students, and I chose Gribovo, a well-known beach in Nafpaktos across the straits. Relaxed group games and swimming had proved popular there. Beachside picturesque restaurants with tables and chairs scattered about under the benevolent shade of giant plane trees presented tempting lunch opportunities.

Years later, while working on my Slavic Linguistics degree, I realized that Gribovo, the name of this favorite spot, is a Slavic word relating to "a place of mushrooms" from "grib," meaning mushroom. Slavic hordes arrived in Greece more than once, beginning in the late sixth century, and were eventually assimilated into the local population. However, to the delight of linguists, a few Slavic words and place names appear here and there.

∞∞∞∞

Most of my students showed up for the Gribovo excursion, and so did Katerina. I rented a small rowboat for my wife and child and invited Katerina to join us.

Was I nuts?

I imagined myself as one of Jason's heroic argonauts, ferrying the Golden Fleece. Only on the bow sat the burden while the precious load was astern, the obligation and the desire, the unwanted and the favorite -- all in one boat, the same little boat floating towards somewhere. I fancied my rowing was as expert as a Venetian gondolier's... My fantasizing mind has always been unrestrained.

I thought of myself as an argonaut...

Katerina soon began forming hearts on the water's surface with some floating leaves. And Olympia took notice, as I found out later, but remained silent.

Weighing anchor

I had succeeded in getting accepted at an American university, saved some money, and readied for departure, but Olympia and my daughter, Carletona, were staying behind. I had to do something with the family before I left. We gave up the two-bedroom house and rented a room where the landlady showed interest in looking after Carletona while Olympia worked as an usherette at a Patras cinema. I left Olympia a small sum and planned to send more from America. I also had high hopes that my parents would relent and take my little family in.

∞∞∞∞

On the day before departure from Greece, Olympia and I said our goodbyes. She may have sensed I was not going back. Although I avoided all indications of that, I knew we were finished. I remember her pretty face while waving goodbye at the doorway. She was despondent but resigned as well. Although she had minimal education, she was intelligent and cunning. She knew how to get her needs fulfilled.

As planned, I rode my moped to Rion to store it in the barn behind the hotel. I spent a few hours with my paternal family as if nothing had ever happened between us, as if that ignominious day of their shameful banning of me had never occurred. They looked at me with an entirely different attitude now. I was no longer the thorn in their side, blaming them for broken promises or asking for educational support; I wanted nothing from them. They likely saw a way to benefit materially from me as I was going to America. I was no longer persona non-grata. If you think this is too cynical an attitude, I suggest the evidence points otherwise.

I was taking the fast train to Athens in the afternoon that day; the railway station was kitty-corner across from Father's house. The whole family walked the short distance to the station with me. My brother carried my only suitcase, and when I mounted the train, he stuck a 1000-drachma bill into my right pocket. I tried to return it, but he insisted on putting it back into my pocket as I climbed the train steps.

One thousand drachmas at that time were about 30 US dollars. The amount was not the focus; I did not want it. My super-bruised pride did not like it.

Why didn't he offer me anything when he visited me at my starving "hole?"

Trouble at the gate

Katerina's father had recently been transferred to an Athens bank during the last couple of months before my departure. I went to their residence to bid them goodbye. Katerina wanted to know where I was staying. I told her, not understanding what she had in mind.

While fantasizing, we can all be imaginative, decisive, audacious, and reckless, but few can take bold action. Katerina showed that she could. Around eleven o'clock that night, when I was already in bed, I heard a knock on my hotel door.

Katerina was standing in front of me with a naughty smile. Joyfully amazed, I let her in, shutting the door quickly behind her. We embraced and kissed, full of love. She quickly removed her clothes except for her panties and jumped in bed. I did likewise. We kissed and kissed and spoke words of burning passion but positively, no more. There was temptation and hardship, but there was iron discipline as well.

There was a well-developed chivalric aspect in me. I determined this was not the time to take advantage of a beloved person on the eve of a planned four-year absence. I explained to her that this was my way of showing her the seriousness of my love. If she could wait, I would get my divorce from Olympia and return to her or bring her to America with me. She understood. She left a couple of hours later.

To appreciate Katerina's surrender to me, one must consider the Greece of 1959. Tradition and practicality demanded that young females be kept under strict control. A marriageable woman's most valuable commodity was her virginity. Safeguarding it was of the utmost importance. Family honor was at stake.

I had already been through one shotgun wedding. I was not going to repeat my teenage mistake. Besides, I was married with a child. A night's escapade could be sacrificed. I was a serious young man with a sacred mission. I was not going to allow anything to interfere with it. Events had put me through great difficulties but had also imparted some wisdom. I believe my action was noble but also wise, and there's reason to be proud.

I went to sleep.

At about two a.m., I heard another knock on my door. *She can't be coming back,* I told myself. Upon opening the door, I was petrified to see Katerina's father! He elbowed his way through as if nothing could stand in his way. We sat down on the bed, and the interrogation began in earnest. He wanted to know one thing: how far we had gone.

"I can have you arrested," he threatened convincingly. "I have contacts with the police. I can ensure you never leave Greece."

My God, not again! I had done everything I knew to get to this point; my boat for America was to leave in the morning. I had to be on that boat.

"I love Katerina," I told him as sincerely and emphatically as possible. "For that reason, I have not touched her," I continued, meaning there had not been any intercourse. "I plan to get my divorce and marry her."

"I understand you have her letters. Give them to me now," my uninvited visitor said, brushing aside my display of rare youthful nobility. With tears running down my face, I walked to my suitcase obediently and took out part of Katerina's letters to me. I handed them to him, letting him think that was all there was. He got up, and without saying another word or shaking hands, he walked out of the

129

room and disappeared behind the closed door as suddenly as he had appeared.

The rest of Katerina's letters are still in the suitcase I brought to America.

Exodus

It took me a lifetime for this day to come. A dream drawn a thousand times, revised, discarded, recovered, and now realized. I had overcome all the obstacles along the way. Neither my parents nor my community's retrograde mentality could hold me back. Not even my own occasional unwisdom could prove fatal. My dream was more powerful than all that taken together. Its constancy provided self-correcting legitimacy. I made it!

The date is September 9, 1959. I am standing on the deck of Queen Elizabeth, one of England's largest passenger ocean liners; the ship is moored at a pier in Piraeus. I am leaning on the side railing along with hundreds of passengers. It is a festive atmosphere; cheerful music is playing for all to hear. People are waving their hands excitedly. A cheering crowd on the pier is waving back. Friends and relatives. Not mine, somebody else's. Words are tossed back and forth, sometimes loud enough to be heard, other times whispered. Multi-colored balloons are hung overhead from a wire running between posts. Lots of confetti paper fragments are strewn about. We will be departing in a couple of hours.

I am going to America! I am going to college! My parents cannot stop me; no one can stop me.

All my material possessions are inside one cheap suitcase. But inside me, innumerable non-material assets are boiling in a cauldron of ambition.

There is so much to learn!

∞∞∞∞∞

More than two thousand people are onboard, all strangers. I am standing on the stern of the huge liner, close to the railing. Alone. For no particular reason, my gaze focuses on the boat's wake. It is solid and well-defined closer to the ship, cutting a straight path, then weakening and dissolving into the vastness of the sea. The land, my motherland, is slowly turning into a blur. Will I ever go back?

VOLUME II: AMERICA

DEMETRIUS KOUBOURLIS PHD

1. Arrival

The Statue of Liberty

It is a misty early morning. Our ship, Queen Elizabeth, is slowly gliding past Liberty Island as if in a majestic procession. I was just awakened by the excited voices of fellow passengers. I'm marveling at the astonishing picture framed by my porthole – the Statue of Liberty!

I had seen pictures of it, to be sure, but this was breathtaking, and it was directly in front of me. It felt as if I could touch it. I looked in awe and rushed to put on some clothes to go out on the deck. Oohing and ahh-ing passengers glued their eyes on the stunning spectacle. "Wow!" gasped a lady in admiration standing beside me at the side railing. As soon as I could tear my eyes away from the enormous statue and focus on the distance, the mounds of skyscrapers seen from afar like sand castles on a Kihei beach filled my horizon. One building was much higher than all the rest -- the Empire State Building.

For a moment, as it was in the very early morning hours, I thought I was still dreaming. Was I? It took a little while for my excitement to settle. I was going into the New World, leaving the old one behind. "This is the Great America, the land of your dreams," I whispered. "Just now, your dreams are fusing with reality." My blood was pulsating; I had finally made it. After years of effort and untold obstacles, I eventually arrived. I was in America; I would be stepping onto its soil shortly. I would be part of this mythic country. I would live and learn.

I was going to have a great life.

New York

Dr. French was to meet me in New York upon my arrival. Indeed, he showed up on the boat before the customs check. I have no idea how he finagled that, but here I was, opening my suitcase for inspection with Dr. French standing beside me on my right.

When the inspector found the garlic Dr. French had asked me to bring for him, it was promptly confiscated. The cookies I had saved off the boat dining table for my bus trip were also heartlessly removed. And so was the homemade cake my calisthenics teacher's wife had prepared for me to give to her nephew in New York City. I have felt sorry ever since for my inability to deliver that cake as promised.

Dr. French tried his diplomatic best to salvage the garlic but to no avail. For some reason, unknown to me, Greek garlic represented magic powers for him; he had made me promise to bring him as much as I could.

I witnessed the bureaucratic implacability and the inflexible rule adherence firsthand. There was no heart. Chances are, some rule-bending would have been expected in Greece, where one could be persuaded ad hominem to crack the hardness. I took note. However, in time, I accepted and even liked this cultural difference. There is nothing wrong with a one-size-fits-all bureaucratic treatment and everything wrong with high-handedness, arbitrariness, underhandedness, and overall unpredictability in dealing with official business that I was familiar with in Greece.

After customs, Dr. French and I, with my sole piece of luggage, walked straight out to where his old Ford was parked. Right away, I became aware of the ambiance of a mystic late morning with the incredible sight of intimidating skyscrapers looming all around and above me. It is hard to describe the feeling of awe, wonder, and admiration for the achievements of what was unfolding in front of my very eyes. I wanted to be part of this great country, grow with it, and hopefully contribute. I had made that vow long before that moment, but an involuntary surge of re-commitment took hold of me. I felt buoyed. I felt levitated. The promised new beginning was afoot. *I was now walking on American soil*!

An anecdotal notion that money is strewn on American streets pervades the Greek mind until one comes to America. As for me, no, I did not look at the roads for scattered dollar bills or coins. However, that attitude fortified persistent claims on the part of friends and relatives left behind that you must send money back as soon as possible and as much as possible. In my experience, hints, requests, and outright demands for cash have amounted to some kind of extortion -- I was no good if I did not conform to this tacit, self-serving rule; I was not a decent relative, true friend, or generous person; I was a tightwad and a disappointment.

The sight of countless skyscrapers thrust at me from all sides, and suddenly, viewed not from a picture or a movie but from the ground you stand on, was breathtaking. I felt transported to a different universe. Soon, my neck started to hurt from looking up and all around. It was surreal.

...countless skyscrapers thrust at me from all sides...

How did they ever build such tall structures? What kind of super-people could conceive and bring to light such bold creations? So much energy, fearlessness, and ingenuity. These were not mere mortals; they must have been Titans, true gods!

I was awestruck.

It occurred to me that the architects and builders, too, must have been people like me, immigrants or descendants of immigrants, who had found a welcome soil and tamed it before it could tame them. I dared imagine myself in great company. I sucked up the sensation and felt urged to join them, to create alongside them, to be part of this great miracle that had unfolded all around me.

"Got to get going, Demetrius!" I heard Dr. French's voice yanking me out of my reverie. "We have a long drive ahead of us."

Trip saga

It took us about 7 hours to cover the more than 400 miles to Salem, WV, where Dr. French lived. That was the first leg on my way to Sacramento, CA. The trip was uneventful; besides stopping to gas up and being introduced to fast food and root beer, I reveled in the sights, and Dr. French rejoiced in introducing me to as much content as possible. My whole being was overflowing with exhilaration; I was filled with enthusiasm and anticipation for my life in the promised land. I was pumped up; I was super-living!

∞∞∞∞

One of my Greek milieu's indisputable "facts" was that Greek law disallowed Greek citizens to leave the country with more than $100 on their person. Everyone was aware of it, and so was I. It was common knowledge, and no one questioned it. With great trepidation before departure, I tried to think of a way to circumvent this law, as more than the allowed amount would be needed for my survival and studies in the States.

Among the few books I had taken with me was an English-Greek dictionary. Its covers were the thickness of ordinary cardboard. Before leaving Greece, I had slit the back cover open, inserted the thousand-drachma bill my brother had stuck into my pocket, and glued the book cover back. I felt it was a fortuitously clever way to circumvent the $100 cash limitation of the supposed Greek law.

∞∞∞∞

When Dr. French decided to leave Greece, he asked for a $500 loan, money he knew I had – I was saving for my trip to America. He promised to return that money to me upon my arrival in the States. Of course, I was glad to assist him – after all, I was so grateful for his help. Also, I thought this was another way to circumvent the 100-dollar Greek legal limitation.

I relied on Dr. French to repay me the $500 loan as I only had the allowed $100 and the Greek 1000-drachma bill in my dictionary's cover.

I was counting on that cash for my survival at the start of my life in America, not to mention the cost of tuition and books. *Dr. French did not offer to return that money.* This was a massive disappointment for me. I could not bring myself to ask for the money.

Because of some inscrutable notion, I sometimes tend to act in a way that is harmful to my interests. It makes no sense. The tragedy only hit me when the bus ticket to Sacramento took 95 of those one hundred dollars! Five dollars was my total liquid fortune to last me all the way to Sacramento. The drachma bill hidden in my dictionary cover was foreign currency and could not be used. The journey ahead of me was 2500 miles with roads that could hardly be compared with today's roads. It took six days and nights to cover the distance.

∞∞∞∞

If there were a contest to cross America from one end to the other, from New York City to Sacramento, with only 5 dollars at one's disposal, I won it. I must have. I was so anxious to reach America that details about how did not matter. I focused solely on stepping on the blessed soil and worried little about worrying. I was filled with a do-now-ask-questions-later attitude that served me well most of the time but would also occasionally get me into some trouble, as it did at this time and later on.

If the food on Queen Elizabeth was abundant and tasty, my nourishment on this road trip was akin to an unplanned hunger strike. I recall the first morning as vividly as if it were today. The Greyhound bus made a breakfast stop. I followed the crowd and took a seat at the counter. I watched the people placing their breakfast orders and tried to figure things out like I had just landed from Mars.

I really did not know anything about American cuisine. It had not been something I was interested in. Besides, I always ate whatever was available for survival. Food was necessary nourishment and nothing else.

So, I studied the situation carefully. The server behind the counter asked for my order. It might as well have been Chinese. Quick thinking came to my rescue.

"Let me have the same as that," I said, pointing at the next person's order and feeling relieved the selection process was terminated immediately. The server quickly obliged but also put a glass of milk alongside.

"I didn't order milk," I said.

"What? Are you going to have your cornflakes without milk?"

"Yes," I said, realizing too late that the milk went with the cornflakes. I was caught in a cultural mini-trap. Either I admitted my ignorance or held on to the integrity of my personal authority.

The real problem was that I was afraid my five dollars would not be enough. I was figuring things out. Besides, I wanted my money to last as long as possible. So, no milk for me. In fact, I was shocked at how much that bowl of dry cereal cost me. I had to make whatever was left of my liquid fortune last me the six-day-long trip to California. Oh, how I missed those Queen Elizabeth cookies that the cruel customs officer confiscated! My mind even flitted to the luscious Greek-American widow's repeated invitations to follow her to Chicago – she offered me free room and board plus tuition for my college. I turned her down. Hunger, yes; gigolo, no!

When the bus made a lunch stop later that day, one passenger did not step off. Ditto for dinner that night. But that lone passenger was amongst the first to exit the bus the following morning. I sat at the counter and ordered my cornflakes WITH MILK! American Gastronomy 101. Check.

Cornflakes with milk, I decided, had to be enough for my survival for the entire trip. As for later, something else would turn up. Besides, someone was picking me up at the bus stop in Sacramento.

∞∞∞∞

The foreign student club of Sacramento State College was well-organized. The club's president and secretary had already written to me. I did not need to worry. The secretary would be meeting me at the bus station upon my arrival. All I would have to do is give her a call.

Sharon Hooker, the club's secretary, came to the bus station in person, in her own car! Sharon had a car! I did not know anyone in Greece who had a car. Sharon, a female, could drive! I did not know a single woman in Greece who could do that. Sharon was my savior at that moment and time.

Oh, America, how great thou art!

I felt the great country was opening its welcoming bosom and letting me in. Intuitive notions invaded my brain, battling my Greek Weltanschauung to death.

Sharon drove me to her house, where I was able to take a shower. I can only imagine my body stench after six days on a bus. I was embarrassed I did not have any clean clothes. On the bus, I had used a handkerchief around my neck to keep my shirt collar from getting too dirty during the long trip. Now was the time to remove that soiled kerchief from my neck and rely on the relatively clean collar to redeem the smelly shirt. She drove me to a Cosmopolitan Club party in someone's apartment. I remember sitting on the carpeted floor and conversing with students from India. They could not believe I had just arrived in the States because of my English.

Sharon proved to be very helpful those first days. I am expressing my gratitude here.

2. Work and Study.

*H**unger in America***
Is it possible for one to go hungry in America? Yes. But it is not for lack of food, as there are several ways to keep some kind of nourishment in one's stomach. The social net can care for many people unless they are dumb or named Demetrius from Greece. Armed with misinformation and enough pride to bend the Statue of Liberty to the ground, I went hungry the first few weeks in America. I was told that foreign students were prohibited from working for the first six months of arriving in the States. My problem was to survive those first six months.

My parents sent me no money. I had left a few hundred dollars in my father's account to get him to sign the American Embassy's papers guaranteeing financial support for me while in America. I kept telling the University's financial officer the money should come any day soon. I had not paid a penny for tuition; I had no money for food, lodging, transportation, tuition, or textbooks. I was penniless and as hungry as it gets.

After my first day following my arrival, Sharon Hooker, the Cosmopolitan Club's Secretary, found a room to rent for me. I took it and was allowed to move in while waiting for "my money." I shared it with a friendly Persian student. I walked or hitchhiked to school for my classes every day. The landlady was a kind lady who invited me to share their table once, but imbecile me waited for an invitation encore to accept. Can you imagine what a hold my culture had on me? My hunger was unbearable. I had visions of starving Jean Valjean, the hero of Les Misérables, stealing a loaf of bread, and I could not help but feel intense empathy for him and his plight.

... *so close, yet very far.*

I recall a lonely piece of cheese my Persian roommate had placed in the fridge. How long I salivated, thinking about that darn morsel is still a sour memory – it was so close, yet very far! He realized I had no food and offered me a small portion. It was indescribably delicious.

I asked around how to cash my thousand drachma bill, which I brought into the US inside the cardboard cover of my Greek dictionary. I went to a bank and timidly presented my treasure. I was escalated to some higher bank official who informed me that the only bank that would exchange it for dollars was in San Francisco. I explained I had no way of going there; could he help? After some reflection and consultation with the bank's manager, he photocopied the bill and suggested I return in a few days. Two days later, I was around inquiring if there was any news. I told the banker I was famished. I needed the money to buy some food. The man's eyes, right there and then, locked with mine, reached for his wallet and offered me ten dollars.

"Consider this an advance on your bill," he said while letting me keep my Greek bill. I entered the first grocery store I came across, my hungry eyes like powerful magnets clicking shut on all edible things. Right away, I realized there was little my treasure could buy. But it was better than nothing. I purchased a carton of powdered milk and determined to ration a glass a day while waiting for some miracle to happen.

My energy level was diminishing daily, but I kept studying while lying in bed on my side to conserve energy. Food was a sine qua non, but education was not far behind. As long as I had water and powdered milk and kept the landlady off my back, I could still prolong my Golgotha.

I went back to the bank on the third and fourth days. Finally, the patient banker informed me my Greek drachma bill was worth 30 dollars, and there would be a conversion fee of about one dollar. Did I want to go ahead with it?

My joy was mixed with disappointment. I thought I could get more, but only an ungrateful fool would look a gift horse in the mouth. The exchange took place, and the ten-dollar loan was paid off. After thanking the good fellow profusely, I went about my way with the rest of my fortune in my pocket.

I never saw that humane banker again, but his deed has remained with me for the rest of my life. I never pass by a beggar without leaving some money, sometimes a surprising amount.

∞∞∞∞

At the college, I made the acquaintance of a black student who was renting a house close to campus with friends. While chatting, I informed him of my plight; he invited me to stay for free at his place while looking for alternatives. I took my leave from my landlady, who probably understood much more than she let on, and told me I owed nothing for the few days I stayed at her house.

A fellow student, a white American, made a joke when he found out I was staying with a black student. He used what I took as a pejorative term whose meaning I did not know.

In my Greek environment, we had no black people. Not even one. When the sixth fleet set anchor in Rion, I met many black sailors for the first time. I had not seen black people in the flesh before. They were friendly young people, no different from the white sailors, looking for booze and something else. My father ensured I supplied them with the former for a fair price.

I recall one time, by the road outside our store, one of the black sailors hurt his foot. I rushed to provide first aid, not paying attention to his color. Other black sailors came around and were delighted I could speak English. Upon finding out I had learned much of my English by reading, they returned the following day with a supply of past issues of Ebony magazine. Beautiful color pictures all over – a first in my experience. I cherished those pages for a long time.

A child's welcome

Meanwhile, back in Greece, events were assuming their own course. My mother was reported to have had a change of heart and got interested in the fate of my child, her first grandchild. Someone told her my little daughter spent a good part of the day alone in the enclosed yard of the rental when my wife, Olympia, had to work. Eventually, my parents decided to take the child to live with them for various reasons.

My parents had retired by this time and had turned their businesses over to my brother. My father had mellowed considerably by this time. The coming of my little child, Carletona, into their lives fulfilled two needs. They had a wonderful, fresh life in their midst and a hook on the emigrated son. From my father's purely calculative point of view, I imagine this was a good deal. However, they all grew to love the child and spoil her regally. My mother knew how to raise her with excellent manners. I surmise that she found out through observation what she did not know. Even the neighbors came to love Carletona, aka Sophia, and treated her with chocolate and other things. She was an intelligent and lovely child who liked to sing and dance. From all accounts, Carletona's life with my parents left nothing to be desired. She proved to be a unifying and revitalizing force.

I kept regular correspondence with them, primarily with my mother, who was a dependable letter writer. At least once a month, she wrote, expressing her love and how she missed me. In one ear for me and out the other. I was too bruised to believe in any expressions of affection, but I did miss them and was anxious to visit.

My plan was to eventually bring my daughter to the States.

A great American

The College's financial office contacted the foreign student's advisor to inquire about my tuition debt. It was at this time that one of those pivotal encounters occurred. The director of the Foreign Students' Office was a wonderful person named Dr. Laurence Brammer. He must have been born for this job. A psychologist by training and a published author, he took a genuine interest in me. I told him everything -- no money was coming. I could not pay for tuition; I was starving and could not secure a place to live. He assured me something would turn up and that he would let me know soon without fail.

I left his office with renewed hope and went to my next class. Everything was going to be alright. I would be allowed to work, have something to eat, and go to school.

Have you noticed how some flies keep coming back to your food? No matter how hard you try to shoo them away, they keep coming until you reach for the swat option. I returned to the foreign student's office when the day's classes concluded. I happened to be passing by, I said. Had the good doctor found something for me?

While getting ushered to the waiting room, I was told Dr. Brammer had some excellent news for me.

"How would you like to live with an American family in exchange for some work?" He asked me. I could tell he felt pleased and proud to be able to offer me that opportunity. He explained that the opening had just come in, and such happened occasionally, but there had not been any openings for quite a while.

My heart was pounding with joy. My problems would soon be over. Dr. Brammer made a call and ascertained that my soon-to-be-hosting lady would be coming in about forty minutes to pick me up. Could I get my stuff ready by then? You bet I could! My brief sojourn with the hospitable black students was going to come to an end. I had been with them for two days and was treated well. They lived near campus, and running there and gathering my stuff in my single suitcase was not a problem.

American family welcome

I was going to live with the Rulisons. Mrs. Rulison came in her spacious station wagon as expected. A mild discomfort invaded me as I got into her car. It is not that she was uncivil or unpleasant or that some foreboding came upon me. It is more likely that I had anticipated some cordiality; after all, I would live in her house. Again, this was a cultural difference. Americans are friendly people, as everyone knows, but are they warm? Greeks are welcoming and exude warmth, sincere or otherwise, but are they genuine?

The car stopped in front of the garage of a beautiful Tudor house in Fair Oaks, a well-to-do Sacramento suburb. I was informed that Dr. Rulison was a busy surgeon in some major downtown hospital and would come home later in the day, provided there were no medical emergencies.

I was awed by doctors then and looked forward to meeting him.

Mrs. Rulison led me into the house and showed me a lovely bedroom downstairs beside the kitchen and dining areas. It came with its own shower. This was going to be my room, she told me. She then presented me to her three children, aged seven to thirteen. She explained I would be expected to babysit whenever necessary. She then took me to the backyard, where a beautiful suburban swimming pool taking up most of the yard engulfed my view. After discovering I had never maintained a pool, she showed me what was needed and emphasized that cleaning had to be done daily. The afternoon was maturing; it was well past 4 o'clock when she finally came to the burning issue:

"I think you can use a bite," she said, looking at me quizzically and placing a sandwich before me. How difficult is it to tell someone is hungry? By just looking? Eyes sunk in, anxious look, shifty glance, meek demeanor, suggestive and amorous glances at the fridge? Dr. Brammer may have filled her in on my condition.

The smell of the cheese pierced my nostrils and blurred my logic. It was no use pretending I was not hungry as good Greek manners would have prescribed.

Like a
hungry
wild
animal

Wasting not a second, like a hungry wild animal, I jumped into my eating orgy. I had not had any decent food for weeks. I grabbed the sandwich and gulped it down in record time while all four Rulisons watched me in dismay. That sandwich was more than exquisite ambrosia to me at that moment; I felt its taste and the gesture's warmth, and it was reassuring; a veil of tension was lifted from my eyes, and a grateful smile graced my face. Before I could thank her, Mrs. Rulison put another sandwich before me. Thank you, Mrs. Rulison!

No, I suppose it is not that hard to tell if someone is genuinely starving.

As I was crunching the second sandwich, I realized that my carefully cultivated eating manners had been thrown out the window. At my parents' restaurant, observing how people ate and drawing conclusions were some of the mind games I indulged in. Soon, I could tell a lot about people by how they ate, like their social status and family background, and even draw more advanced conclusions as to whether they had been abused in their family. Of course, these were my private observations and suppositions and lacked scientific status. Yet, as I have gone through life, I have come to appreciate how valuable such supplementary education has been.

"I apologize for eating fast," I said as if I was coming to. "Truth is, I haven't had a decent meal for some time."

My parents might have been ashamed of me at that moment. I was committing a behavioral blunder; I was apologizing. The Greeks of my time and place were not good apologists. An apology was perceived as a sign of weakness, or so it was thought. People would go to great lengths to stick to their right or wrong position to protect their authority and sacred status in the community.

Yet, admitting error, I have come to believe, is one of man's nobler manifestations. Lamentably, one occasionally learns of people in responsible positions who slaughter the truth to protect their precious stance of consistency.

∞∞∞∞

Life with the Rulisons was smooth. While personal warmth was missing, a proper relationship nevertheless flourished. Dr. Rulison even took me to the neighbors one weekend to see the first color TV in the neighborhood. I was in awe of the technology but never had time for TV while studying at the university.

I did my daily chores dutifully – the most challenging part was dealing with the kids when the parents were away. They proved to be very difficult. I was not prepared for that. I had my culture's means of dealing with children, which I clearly could not and would not employ. So, I was on my own. The rebelliousness of the boy tested my limits. I did not know what to do with him.

There came a time when Mrs. Rulison took some interest in my personal life. Sharon Hooker, the Cosmopolitan Club Secretary, who had helped me upon my arrival in Sacramento, would call from time to time to chat. Mrs. Rulison asked me why I was not asking Sharon out. She did not know I was married and had a beloved in Greece or that my principal love was learning. And that I was somehow principled, or so I fancied. However, I surmised she began thinking I was gay.

She maintained that I should respond to Sharon's advances. A date was set, and Sharon took me to a movie. Later, another beautiful 18-year-old lady spotted me in the cafeteria and asked a mutual acquaintance to ask me out. This was my second date in America. We went to a movie. Both dates picked me up in their car, but there was no sequel to either date. This must have convinced Mrs. Rulison I was gay. Soon, she decided the time had come for me to move out. Such is life.

A few years later, while visiting Sacramento, I stopped to see the Rulisons. Mrs. Rulison shared her pain with me. There were behavioral problems with her son. She asked my advice, wanting to know how "you people" handle this. I saw clearly she still thought I was gay despite the fact I had my American wife with me during the visit.

No, thank you.

Living with the Rulisons took care of my room and board, but some cash was needed for other expenses such as tuition, textbooks, etc. I returned to the Foreign Students' Office, asking Dr. Brammer for help.

"Can you do gardening?" he asked me.

"Of course," I said, although I hardly had any idea as I had never done it.

"How about Saturday, the day after tomorrow?" He suggested.

"Sure," I responded eagerly.

"I'll pick you up at eight in the morning," he said. He already knew where or could get my address from his records – after all, he had placed me there himself a couple of days earlier.

I worked very hard that day. That was my chance to make a good impression. I remember my lower back hurting a lot, but I kept working as hard as possible without taking a break. I felt this was my opportunity to show gratitude and secure steady employment.

After a few hours, Dr. Brammer came outside to show me what else needed to be done and suggested I slow down. "The neighbor called me," he said. "He's wondering if you could also work for him. He's never seen anyone work as hard as you."

I knew the dart had hit the bull's eye. I kept telling myself that *no matter what the opportunity, do your best. You will be noticed. You will make it.*

Lunchtime was nearing, and Mrs. Brammer asked me if I was ready for lunch.

"No, thank you," I said, expecting a repeat of the offer. This was the polite way to respond in my culture. However, the proposal was not repeated as the rules of a different culture were in operation. Mrs. Brammer may have assumed I had prepared my own lunch and went about her business. I kept working as I did not know garden workers would take a break for lunch. Dr. Brammer came out after a while and asked if I wanted to eat lunch.

"No, thank you," I responded again, as this was a resetting of the offer made by a different person. And I went about my frenetic work performance until about five when Dr. Brammer came out of the house again, saying:

"Quitting time. Let me give you a ride home."

"No, thank you," I responded, again expecting a sequel to the offer. I got paid, and off I walked, ignoring my growling stomach and nursing my ailing back. But the incident did not end there. Eventually, both the Brammers and I figured out what had transpired. Our two cultures had been clashing. I had expected an "insistent" invitation. The faulty thinking went like this: it is not polite to show eagerness in such cases; instead, let the other person repeat the offer; then, you know they mean it, and you avoid showing bad manners. However, the insistent invitation never came. In American culture, I later understood that if someone says "No, thank you," it means just that. It is not an opening for a tug-and-pull dialog.

More opportunities to meet with the Brammers surfaced. They took me along on a trip to San Francisco. Dr. Brammer asked me to teach his family some French, which I did. The Brammers got so interested in me that they even visited my parents in Greece! Many years later, while walking to one of my graduate classes at the University of Washington, I ran into Dr. Brammer. He was now on the faculty there! The last time we had seen each other was in Sacramento. Over the decades, we met a few more times. The Brammers even took part in the wedding of one of my daughters, where many of Seattle's crème de la crème attorneys were present – one of my Harvard lawyer daughters was getting married. The Brammers wasted no time telling anyone within hearing distance about my humble beginnings and the meaning of "No, thank you" in Greek.

Every time we met, Dr. Brammer or Marne, his wonderful wife, would recite the days of the week in French as I had taught them and repeat our "No, thank you" story amidst heartfelt laughter. Mrs. Brammer would always apologize for not repeating her invitation on that fateful, culture-caused starvation day.

I asked one of my professors, Dr. Skalbeck, if he needed some gardening done. After all, I was an expert gardener by now. I worked most of one Saturday and would not accept money as the man had been very helpful to me with the language lab. Despite his repeated insistence, I did not take the money, although, God knows, I needed it. This was my way of paying back and showing gratitude.

Like many students, I had to work to pay for my living and school expenses. As my debts increased, holding more than one summer job became necessary. Tuition and other debts had to be paid; the financial office began dunning me gently. One summer, I held four part-time jobs.

Second class

After Mrs. Rulison asked me to seek alternative quarters, I returned to the Foreign Students' Office with my renewed plight -- I needed a place to live. Fortunately, a few American families were now looking for foreign students to help with the household chores.

Mrs. Woo, an American-Chinese widow, had a lovely house in Sierra Oaks, the same area as the Rulisons. She needed someone to help vacuum, wash the dishes, and do chores around the home. I moved right in. Once, she asked me to take her Cadillac to change the oil. I had no license and only a few lessons, but I relished the opportunity to drive a Cadillac. Fortunately, I was able to complete the task without incident but with enormous trepidation.

Sometimes, I take chances for the thrill of it. Perhaps one should not.

I tried my best to adjust to Mrs. Woo's peculiarities. She never smiled. I felt intentionally distanced and was treated like a second-class citizen. Although she prepared our meals, she insisted on eating alone in the large dining room while I ate in the adjacent kitchen at the same time. I was made to feel like a plebeian. Her overall treatment of me was off-putting, but I had enough experience, patience, and motivation to get along. I found it hard to respect her in return but had no trouble satisfying the requirements perfunctorily. Some people feel more important and accomplished if they keep another human in indebted servitude.

I learned over the years the importance of treating people with respect, no matter how lowly their position. As a society, we can get along much further through a consistent practice of mutual respect.

MS patient's equal

Another of my live-in jobs was taking care of a Multiple Sclerosis patient. It was dreadful to witness what MS can do to a human body. The man was skin and bones. My job was to lift him from his bed to the bathroom and to the dinner table as needed. He had been a successful executive in a Sacramento company. His lovely house was evidence of that. His wife and daughter lived in the house as well.

Taking care of an invalid was a humbling experience for me. The patient and I quickly became friends. When he learned about my lexical abilities, he asked for his Webster's English Dictionary to be placed on the table beside his plate. After meals, he would randomly look up words and ask me about their origin. He was amazed I could answer most of them correctly. We had a good time playing this game together. I enjoyed it quite a bit because I could bring a smile to his face. Human warmth was missing from the two previous live-in experiences. I instinctively looked for that, for some closeness, some you-are-one-of-us-ness, and his treatment of me did that. I wonder if his ailing condition, by increasing his dependence, had allowed a better side of him to surface.

Another job was helping make and decorate cakes. As I was artistically inclined, learning the basic skills did not take long. The owner, an old Swedish immigrant, was affable and took pleasure in showing me the tricks of the trade.

No, I am not available for cake decorations.

Still, another job was selling shoes for a chain shoe store. The manager did not like using my name over the store loudspeaker system when directing me to serve a customer. My name's "foreignness" would put off the parochial suburbanites, who would not feel comfortable and might not shop -- that must have been the rationale. He decided my name would be 'Mr. D." OK. Whatever. I had to put on my best clothes and behave as if in a church.

You must do what you need to do.

Donuts delivery

Probably the most memorable and short-lived job was driving a donut delivery vehicle. I did not reveal I had never driven a truck, nor was I asked about it. There was a problem, however: I did not know how to shift gears, so I used the first gear and managed to deliver the donuts on time until one day when I did not. I failed to hear the 5 a.m. alarm clock to wake up as my other part-time jobs left little time for sleep. My boss got angry at me for missing the delivery and fired me immediately. Although he owed me a week's wages, he refused to pay because he had lost customers with my missed delivery. He decided, he said, to become a monk and made it clear it was because of me. To this day, I have not figured out why monasticism was the logical consequence of my failure to deliver donuts. Had I known that, I might have been motivated to do a better donut delivery job.

The Governor's cameraman

Another extremely short-lived job was serving as a cameraman for one of the Sacramento TV channels. At the time, I was the college's French Professor's reader and helped French language students with their language laboratory needs. Thanks to this association with the audio-visual laboratory, I was asked to be the TV cameraman when a downtown TV channel's staff fell ill. I said I had never done that. The man assured me there was nothing to it. You do this, and you do that, he said convincingly. You'll do fine. I was to present myself at ten a.m. on Saturday at the Sacramento Capitol.

The subject of my virgin filming career was none other than Pat Brown himself, the then governor of California. All went well with the preparation, and I was assigned Camera Two. The crew director would decide which camera to turn on during the show, and he would choose from one of the two cameras. When he called my camera number over the headphones, I was supposed to follow directions to the letter, pointing the camera as instructed. Without any experience whatsoever, I must have been the quickest study in film-making history. There was a problem, however. It took me a while to steady the gigantic camera, which made the governor look shaky and aggravated the crew director. Everything went OK once I got the hang of it. Only later did it occur to me that the person who had recommended an inexperienced cameraman such as myself for this job might have been a Republican, eager to embarrass the Democratic governor.

I was never invited back. This was as close to Hollywood as I ever got.

Fuller Brush stardom

No doubt, the most profitable and least time-consuming job was as a Fuller Brush salesman. Selling was not complex for me as I had grown up in a business environment, had helped run my father's grocery store, and had graduated from a business school. I bought a Vespa and scootered around the suburban neighborhoods, picking up orders one could place from a Fuller Brush catalog I carried with me. The company supplied its salespeople with "free samples" of high-markup items to gain access to people's homes. Housewives were usually polite and, at times, welcoming. But occasionally, husbands would shoo me away with a broom before I could get near the front door. One rare time, a fellow even pulled a gun on me!

A write-up in the local paper featuring me seated on my Vespa helped open many doors. People became more welcoming, and the money kept coming in. However, I could not work more than a few hours each Saturday as the job drained me. I did not like it. Before long, I had too many orders to deliver with my Vespa. I hired someone with a station wagon for the deliveries.

A few hours of work each Saturday was enough to support me for a while.

During a Fuller Brush conference in the greater Sacramento Fuller Brush area, the district manager asked me to climb on top of a table and tell everybody how I had managed to sell so many bottles of insecticide. He had seen my impressive sales figures and was intrigued. Of course, I was unaware of this bit of salesmanship, but I was glad to share my homemade presentation.

Good salesmen are practical people with a good understanding of the human psyche. Either you have that ability, or you do not. Many people have some of that, but thankfully, most do not.

American Maintenance.

One of my first night jobs for American Maintenance, a janitorial company, was picking up the garbage and sweeping the floors at an elementary school. I could not wait to finish the cleaning in record time so I could read as many of the beautifully designed books stacked all around me as possible. I had never seen so many attractive colors. I would sit on the floor between the book racks and dive in. Books have always been my best friend. They fascinate, guide, and inspire me.

Another night job with American Maintenance was cleaning an extensive suite of offices in downtown Sacramento. The foreman, a sturdy Portuguese immigrant, took a liking to me when he discovered we could communicate, he in his native Portuguese and I in my bookish Italian. Probably thinking it would help me, he bought a Portuguese dictionary, which he gave me as a present. However, he once caught me studying the dictionary under one of the office desks. I apologized and explained that, as he could see, I had already finished my required work – I was assigned what was thought to be an eight-hour job but could quickly finish in half that time. He smiled and allowed me to do that regularly!

Don't let the others see you!

"But don't let the others see you," he warned. I always brought that Portuguese dictionary to work with some class worksheets inside.

The good foreman was probably flattered that I showed an interest in his mother tongue, and he might not have noticed I was taking advantage of his kindness.

∞∞∞∞

Probably the unhealthiest job I was ever given with American Maintenance was cleaning a large, hangar-like hall used for union meetings. There were hundreds of metal folding chairs, and the floor was packed with stomped cigarette butts. It reeked heavily of tobacco. I can only imagine the quality of air with so many people smoking at the same time. We have come a long way as a society, I believe, with banning cigarette smoking. However, I cannot understand why it took so long.

∞∞∞∞

I recall another job cleaning the cafeteria on the 21st floor of the Sears Building in downtown Sacramento. My job was to mop the floor daily and clean away all trash. The task took a long time. It was like robbing me of my most precious resource: learning time. Anything that took me away from books felt like the enemy. But I had to earn a living, make money to survive, and pay for my education. I had to *earn it myself.* I devised a simple way to do some of both. Using some copper wire, I made a contraption to hold a two-by-four-inch card with notes in front of me, typically unknown words, and attached it to the long handle, a mop, or a swimming pool vacuuming handle. While rhythmically moving the handle back and forth, I practiced the words in my mind. Tasks like swimming pool vacuuming or floor-mopping were very dull for me. I perceived them as spirit-killing.

Those night jobs were not the best for my mind, spirit, or body, but what choice did I have? Oh, how I missed sleeping enough those days! I recall being invited to a foreign students' party in a park once. With my date sitting on a patio chair, I lay on the grass beside her and slept all through the party fun. I was starved for sleep.

∞∞∞∞

Once, my caring foreman asked me:

"Want to make some extra bucks?" Before I could respond in the affirmative, he explained it was for the coming Saturday, and the pay would be time and a half. I was not familiar with this system at that time.

"Be here at 8 a.m. this Saturday," he said.

And so, it was. I joined a dozen men on a company bus for a job outside Sacramento. We were to strip and mop the floors of a small suburban bank branch. As soon as we arrived, I began working assiduously as was my wont. The foreman wasted no time taking me aside:

"Take it easy, mate," he said. "This job is to last eight hours for all of us."

Hello Demetrius! Welcome to Labor Syndication. Although the pay was good that day, many new thoughts invaded my consciousness, and questions were raised.

The following week, I was asked to join a line of picketers. I had no idea what that was all about, but I refused to go as I did not have time. I got fired on the spot.

My first wheels

The Brammers always tried to find ways to assist foreign students. They were a couple dedicated to helping and entertaining foreign students. They were unique people who were well-disposed towards their fellow humans, always looking for ways to be of assistance. For me, they represent excellent examples of Americans and human beings.

You will recall Dr. Brammer helped me find a place to live and get a job. He and his wife visited my parents in Greece and saw my little daughter. As if that were not enough, the Brammers gifted me their aging Nash, a popular fifties car, long no longer in production. They went even further than that. Mrs. Brammer gave me some driving lessons. However, in the end, because they feared it would cost me a lot to keep the car in running condition or witnessed some discouraging signs of anemic driving alertness in me, the good people decided it was best to sell the vehicle and give me the money instead.

I got 26 dollars from the sale of my first car before I could even own it!

For a song

While waiting in line at the Sacramento State College cafeteria one day, I heard someone from the kitchen area whistling "Samiotisa," a well-known traditional Greek tune. As no one could be seen behind the display case, I called out in Greek: "Eh, Samiotisa, where are you?" I must have astonished the people in line around me by appearing to utter loud gibberish out of the blue. Right away, a young, short, and well-fed fellow with an unmistakable Hellenic face came out all smiles. We began a lively conversation across the display case in Greek, like long-lost cousins nonchalantly invading the hearing space of all bystanders. We got together several times later. He gave me some driving lessons with his brand-new red Chevrolet and helped me get my driver's license, all thanks to Samiotisa.

Culture can unite or set us apart; a whistled tune broadcast a signal; it elicited some human warmth and struck up a friendship. Indeed, people from any nation experience a pleasant feeling upon casually running into compatriots. The smaller the country, the more intense the feeling since the chances for an encounter are rarer and far less expected.

Similarly, paying attention to accents has been my biggest acquaintance-mining tool. I never hesitate to guess the country of origin, and I frequently start a conversation using the person's language if I know it. It is a lot of fun and a life-enhancing experience.

3. Sacramento State College

*C*osmopolitan Club
Beginning with the second semester at Sacramento, my participation in the Cosmopolitan Club, a foreign student association, grew as if by itself due to the significant number of students from various countries and my genuine interest in foreign languages. Somehow, I was noticed, and it was suggested I was "a natural for the task." My name was put up for President, and I was easily elected. It was no problem relegating my responsibilities and organizing exciting and entertaining events despite my lack of experience. My name was put up semester after semester, and I won every time. I have fond recollections from special occasions organized by my fellow foreign students for my birthdays.

One occasion stands out. During one of the club elections, a serious issue emerged. Several students challenged the scope of the club. They claimed it should be exclusively for foreign students and Americans should not be admitted. I had to argue against this so obviously unacceptable stance. It was like saying that foreign students came to America to avoid meeting Americans. Absurd! I won.

MISIRLOU

Cosmopolitan Club,
Sacramento State College

Once, we arranged a campus-wide ethnic dinner gala attended by a couple of hundred people. Various delicious dishes were prepared by our foreign students; entertainment featured a musical presentation by our very own four-member "band," including yours truly as the guitar soloist. I recall the lasting applause after we played "Misirlou," a tune from the Eastern Mediterranean. Although I thought very little of my rendition, I got a bit of the taste that big stars experience following the enthusiastic applause and witnessing a few people lining up to chat with me after the performance.

On another occasion – it must have been my last year at the college – the Cosmopolitan Club arranged our biggest show under my direction. It included many more national dishes and a series of shows and was attended by our largest crowd. I served as the MC and took part in a couple of the performances. Fellow students joked I should head for Hollywood, but I had other plans.

Even the College President was present. In fact, he sought me out after the event, put his arm around my shoulder, and praised our production profusely several times. Not being the kind to miss an opportunity, I pleaded with the President to help reduce the Foreign Students' tuition, as it was double the norm. He patiently explained what a good deal we foreign students were getting and that the actual cost was much higher. Although he didn't convince me then, I now have no problem seeing how right he was.

Student Council

I must have made an unusual impression on some people around me. They must have seen me sprinting from class to class and noticed I was always in a hurry. To save time, I would pack my classes close together so that I could leave campus for work. Consequently, I would sprint from class to class to be on time. A Classics aficionado even made jokes likening me to Hermes, the winged runner.

Another fellow student looked at me with entirely different eyes. He decided to promote my candidacy for the Student Council, specifically as the Humanities Representative of the college. On his own, he created signs and posted them in strategic spots around campus: "VOTE FOR THE NOBLE GREEK. Demetrius for the Humanities." I did not make any speeches or appearances and simply went along for the ride. I did not think anything would come of it, but I won decisively and served the entire year. As the college's Humanities Representative, I was even sent to San Francisco to participate in a three-day political event headed by Jerry Brown, the future governor of California and a two-time presidential candidate. His father was the Governor of the state at the time. You will recall that I had previously filmed the Governor when I was hired to fill in for a sick cameraman.

Minimally, this whole experience taught me that I was not cut out for political life, no matter what my fellow students thought of my abilities. It is probably due to my liking to do things rather than talking about doing them.

Orientation Leader

The college would appoint half a dozen upperclassmen yearly to serve as Orientation Leaders. I was picked for the task one time. This was not a paying function; it was an honorary one. I met my designated group in one of the college's large classrooms at the appointed time.

No one told the orientation leaders what to say; we were on our own. Anyway, I had long before discovered that I had no trouble talking to large groups of people. I aimed to acquaint incoming students with our college and be entertaining.

This event would not be worth mentioning unless one considers the presence of an incoming freshman who was to profoundly affect my life.

English classes

Every foreign student at Sacramento State College was obligated to take a minimum of a year's course on the English language. That was a reasonable requirement. My advisor guided me into that course as was prescribed. Numerous international students were in the class, but soon, linguistic exchanges between Dr. McCullough, the professor, and myself took up much of the hour. After a few days, the professor took me aside:

"You don't belong in this class. Your English is much more advanced. I've talked to Dr. Enroth, and we think his class would be a better fit for you." It was a seminar on W.B. Yeats, an Irish poet and playwright. I could not tell if my English professor wanted to rid himself of me or acted in my best interest. However, it was a fortuitous move as I developed an excellent relationship with Dr. Enroth and took yet another class from him.

Crispus and Fausta

As if working to put me through school and pursuing a respectable class load were not enough, I translated a novel by my student and friend, Christos Anastasopoulos (now Chris Poulos). My young friend had proven to be an able writer. He wrote *Crispus and Fausta*, a captivating story published in serial form in *Peloponissos*, a still circulating Patras newspaper. There were no translation tools in those days other than dictionaries, so the task proved very laborious.

As my English translation needed polishing by a skilled English native, I turned to Dr. Enroth, my Yeats professor. He agreed to do the work, not realizing how much time it would require. After about fifty pages, he gave up, and with time, so did I. The English version of the book never saw the light of publication. Sorry, Chris.

Precious counsel

While working on my B.A. degree in Sacramento, I faced a career decision-making crisis. There was no problem the first year as the courses were of the general requirement kind. However, when it came time to declare my major, my father interjected his despotic interference. He was pressuring me to study engineering. He evidently heard that someone's son in the community was planning to become, or had become, an engineer and that a lot of money would be made in that career.

My father, who had done everything in his power to prevent me from getting an education, was now presuming to dictate the direction of my studies. Moreover, he had not, and was not, providing me with any financial support whatsoever. Still, he felt empowered to insist on his career choice for me. He wanted me to study engineering or else.

I was conflicted. I did not even question my father's right to make such a demand upon me. I talked to my advisor, who happened to be the Cosmopolitan Club's faculty representative – I was the Club's President then. He was a physics professor.

"No problem, you can take my courses. Physics and Chemistry." He also designated Algebra, Calculus, and Mechanical Drafting.

I followed the advice and registered for these courses. It was horrible advice as I did not have an adequate background in these subjects. I found them extremely interesting but challenging. I must have been at the bottom of the class -- this was a new feeling for me. I was utterly miserable. I felt disoriented and began losing sleep.

One of the other classes was French. I enjoyed it and was good at it. The professor liked me, and after testing my Italian (is there a connection?), he made me his assistant.

One of my French classmates, Jim Algeo, also had a strong interest in French. We soon became friends as we were both interested in and good at languages. I told him about my plight, my father's insistence on studying engineering, and how miserable I was with my engineering track classes.

Christmas break came around.

"Why don't you come with me over Christmas? My parents would love to meet you." he blurted out unexpectedly. We traveled in his car from Sacramento to Sonoma. I liked his parents' rustic house. I had never been in a home of that style. Jim's parents treated me like a member of the family. In fact, for every Christmas present Jim was given, there was also one for me. (I had never been given Christmas presents, believe it or not. Well, almost. Our father once gave each of us four children a five-drachma coin to celebrate the holy days. However, he took the coins back the following day!)

∞∞∞

During our walks in and around this beautiful small California town, Jim confidently advised me to drop out of those courses and devote my energy and talents to languages because I had a passion that made me feel fulfilled and engaged; that put me at the top of the class, not the bottom; that took away stress, and capitalized on my core values with which my father's cold calculations had no relationship.

Humanities or exact sciences? Many of us confront this dilemma. College programs indeed take this into account. In the first two years, one is guided to take general interest courses and get acquainted with various fields of study before deciding.

"There aren't too many of us," Jim said, referring to our better-than-average language aptitude. Indeed, we were at the top of the class. (He later received his doctorate and became a Romance Linguistics Professor, and I became a Slavic Linguistics Professor).

When we returned to Sacramento, I gathered my courage and visited my advisor. I let him know of my decision. He was unhappy but understood and helped me chart a new study path. With my career direction established, I embarked on a heavy language load, and wasting no time, I even completed two correspondence courses from the University of California, Berkeley -- Russian and Italian.

∞∞∞∞

After changing my major, I informed my father that I had given up the engineering track and listed my reasons. Without wasting time, he wrote back that he was immediately disowning me and discontinuing all contact. Subject closed.

This created a profound psychological turmoil in me. I was caught between a rock and a hard place. Before I could recover from one upheaval – my choice of major, I crashed into another as I wanted to please my father and follow my own star. "Disowning" me from his assets had no effect on me. It was the moral disowning that wreaked havoc in my vulnerable soul.

For years, I could not understand how my father could maintain such a powerful moral hold on me and, quite surprisingly, how he could get so much cooperation from me to my detriment.

"Honor thy father and thy mother," goes the fifth commandment (Exodus 20:12). That message and the rest of the commandments were pounded in me at school, church, and home. Nowadays, I have no trouble giving it a label. Children, maybe not all, are like putty in the hands of their parents and their culture. Any message, especially if repeated often enough, receives permanent status and becomes unquestioned. I was brainwashed. A country's citizens are also subject to the same indoctrination technique, whether social or political.

Right turns

One never knows how a chance encounter may turn out. This is the exciting unpredictability of meeting people from various backgrounds and countries. Most of our meetings have no real significance -- they come and go, but something momentous gets occasionally seeded. Such were my encounters with Dr. French, Mr.

Psaros, Mr. Pitas, occasional hotel guests, Dr. Brammer, and Jim Algeo, among others. I could not have known or suspected how these encounters would or could turn out. Indeed, none of these people had any inkling our paths would cross and that they would unwittingly have a pivotal influence on my life. Most of them were unaware that their appearance in my life's path had such a beneficial effect. This is what luck is.

In my turn, I have been repeatedly told that I have influenced the lives of others positively. This gratifies me greatly. Hopefully, my voyage through life has not been vacuous.

Indeed, no man is an island. Whatever we have made of ourselves could not have occurred in a vacuum. The social infrastructure, like the physical infrastructure, has been in place. I am deeply grateful to my benefactors and anyone else for their intended or fortuitous contribution to improving my life.

4. Not without Eve

Katerina

The first year in Sacramento, away from what had been my life, was challenging. I cannot say I missed my wife, parents, or my homeland, but I did indeed miss my friends and, most of all, my infant daughter.

And I missed Katerina terribly for the first few months after arriving in the States. You will recall Katerina was my platonic beloved when I left Greece. We corresponded through General Delivery a couple of times. Then, my letters started coming back. It was painful.

I asked Thomas R., a former student and friend of mine, who was with the tourist police in Athens, to find out. He reported seeing her getting on a bus. She looked lost, he told me. I do not know how much value to put into this, but he could or would do nothing more.

I also asked Chris P., another former student and friend, if he could help. He tried. When I returned to Greece after getting my B.A. four years later, I looked for Katerina again, but in vain. I stopped looking on subsequent trips to Greece. I had given up. Then, more than half a century later, the desire to find her and discover what had happened to her resurfaced. The internet was not much help. The people who sounded like her children or relatives did not respond. I created a social network account in the hope of finding her. She would be an old lady, white-haired and probably overweight if alive. What did I expect to gain from such a contact? Fill some gaps, reminisce like an old sentimental fool? One can suppose it would be exciting and could rekindle a friendship. I am not fooling myself, though. What we had in our youth can never be re-captured, just like our past is gone and cannot be had again -- it vaporized, turning into a memory, no different from so many other memories our lives create.

Jeannie

When I realized Katerina would never be part of my life, other females silhouetted in my consciousness. It is always the same for all; people of opposite sexes are naturally intended to attract each other. We are social animals with pre-programmed biological needs. Of course, obstacles that may interfere with this normal process include religion.

In a primarily monotheistic culture, religion is tightly intertwined with culture; it is not possible to separate the two. I was raised in the Greek Orthodox tradition, like most Greeks of my time. An undeniably cultural homogeneity was inevitable. However, a different behavioral paradigm confronted me when I immigrated to a multi-religious, multicultural society. Other moral and ethical guidelines were facing me. Polytheistic cultures tend to be more flexible, but monotheistic societies are nothing but. Inflexibility engenders uncompromisingly authoritative attitudes, entrenching themselves deeper into the core of society. There seems to be an all-or-nothing control over all aspects of life.

I was a product of such a culture and may have been unaware of it. When everyone thinks alike, there is no room for questioning. One accepts the situation as the norm; one does not question it but reacts decisively against anyone who does. Reading world literature must have exposed me to different ways of thinking, unlike the unconcerned man on the street, steeped in a centuries-old tradition that left no room for doubt.

Homogeneity had solidified. I recall more than once how I was viewed as an apostate every time I dared voice what I considered an enlightened opinion. However, it must be said that there was never a fanatical aspect to religion around me in Greece.

I recall one incident in particular: my father and I engaged in a quasi-intellectual-religious discussion. If you think this statement is oxymoronic, consider yourself closed-minded. I must have been 14-15 years old. After one of my deductive readings of the New Testament, I presented some of its contradictions to my father. He listened to me carefully, not showing any emotion. But when I got done, he erupted with a verbal outburst I had not experienced up to that time.

"You're the Antichrist; get out of my house!"

I was astounded by his reaction and felt threatened. I intended my presentation to inform and impress my father with my "erudition." His outburst was undoubtedly a temporary hyperbole as life in his house continued as before. Was he acting out of godly fear? Was he anxious to disassociate himself from the "antichrist" and keep his house sanctified?

Religions aim to provide guidance, whether one wants it or needs it. Most people can ill afford to be without some kind of moral guidance, whether "divine" or organizational. Military training provides a set of behavioral rules and can coexist with monotheistic or polytheistic societies. Like it or not, religions have a far-flung reach in society and politics. Monotheistic cultures are more exclusive and less tolerant of nonstandard behavior than Polytheistic societies. Conformity is the goal. Personal freedom in moral matters can be perceived as less valued in a monotheistic environment. The teachings and rules of a single deity influence society, demanding strict adherence.

My gradual unofficial distancing from the church at about age 15 did not mean I divested myself of my culture -- a virtually impossible task. It meant I stopped going to church and pushed religion to the background. I grew out of it but carried an undeniably religious upbringing inside me. This was inevitable as my 12-year primary and secondary schooling included a religious lesson each day for six days each week, not to mention the family environment and the regular religious rituals and festivals. Taken together, this amounted to an indoctrination of the first magnitude.

My coming to America exposed me to a polytheistic society, which encouraged a more tolerant modus vivendi. In the Greece of my time and place, there was no choice as to which god to listen to and which set of beliefs, customs, and social rules to adhere to.

Such was my mental baggage when I started to date a Catholic girl in America. We were attracted to each other in a genuinely wholesome way, believing a long-term relationship lay before us. Jeannie was comfortable with her faith's existence in a polytheistic environment. She had grown up in it and may have hoped and expected that I would "convert." Such a concept did not exist in my cultural makeup. I had not known anyone who converted, and I did not imagine such would be a factor in my life until it became. From my history reading, I learned of religious persecutions and forced conversions. However, I had no personal experience or knowledge of it. Religious differences were not going to be a factor in my life. Jeannie knew I was raised as a Greek Orthodox and had not practiced religion for many years. She must have wondered about the future. My guess is that she must have counted on my eventual conversion. Our relationship progressed normally. A great affection flourished between us, exempt from intimate contact other than necking.

In intimate relationships, absolute truth has always been one of my desiderata. I have always striven to be truthful and expected my partner to reciprocate. So, I laid my heart bare; I told Jeannie about my marriage, daughter, and plans. She seemed to go along with it, and our relationship proceeded with great affection until she decided to consult with her church's priest. The verdict was merciless: she had to break the relationship immediately!

Furthermore, the relationship was "sinful" and had to be stopped with some absolution penalties for Jeannie. The circumstances, the affection, and the budding love between us did not matter. The canonical edict brooked no flexibility. It was cut and dry. I was crushed to learn of this. What was supposed to guide moral behavior interfered with our lives.

The question of asking "my priest" for personal advice was alien to me. I was religiously emancipated. While I respected Jeannie's religious beliefs, as I have always advocated for all, I bemoaned that our beautiful relationship had to end because it contradicted her sacred canon.

As for me, I preferred to rely on the logic of a given situation. In this case, we were two young people with a great affinity for each other. And here comes a *deus ex machina* messing it all up. I was likely perplexed and angered about this. Why had Jeannie not told me from the start that this was one of her conditions? From the beginning, she knew about my Greek wife and that we were divorcing. I felt betrayed.

I did not let any of this interfere with my education. Indeed, there was emotional turmoil, but by now, I was getting familiar with "female" issues. It had to be processed, like it or not, painful or not. Jeannie wanted to be "friends" and continue our relationship. I did not know her ultimate aim, but soon, another female crossed my horizon.

Maria

Maria was one of my Greek American Cultural Institute students in Patras who had requested private lessons. She was a few years my senior. One day -- I do not remember why -- I was giving her a ride on my moped. We flirted with each other in jest, but nothing came of it. Soon, I left Greece. Some time afterward, she took the initiative to find my address and write. A friendly correspondence developed.

Under some intricate circumstances and by some congressional ruling, she was admitted to the US and was studying at some small college in the eastern United States, she wrote. The correspondence continued for several months; she would relate details about her life and how no good men were to be found in her circles. Growing older, she must have been panicking as she had not cornered her man. Soon, she expressed the desire to transfer to Sacramento State College and asked for my help. Of course, I helped her apply and register. I also located a room for her in the same house I was renting. It was the home of a retired Greek locomotive engineer.

Maria was a vibrant extrovert and an excellent dancer. She had gotten her Arthur Murray certificate and soon got connected with a local branch. On a Saturday, we went out to a night spot. We danced a lot. Then another night again. In the middle of that night, she slipped into my room totally uninvited and unexpectedly. The landlord and his wife, sleeping only an indoor door away, heard the indicative noises and, the following day, told us point-blank we had to find alternative quarters.

Which we did.

After living together for a while, we discovered we were incompatible. For one, Maria proved to be a big flirt on the dance floor during the Cosmopolitan Club parties. I took it as an insult that my girlfriend would flirt with other men, especially in my presence, and told her to stop it. But she could not help it.

"Go find yourself another girlfriend." She told me some time later. Without wasting much time, I moved out. I would see her occasionally on campus between classes.

One day, while exiting one of my classes, I found her waiting for me outside the classroom door. She needed to talk. She was sweating more than usual and had a panicked expression. Without any introductory remarks, she informed me she was pregnant.

It is the same old story. This was the classic ensnaring technique. The male idiot usually co-operates in this, and so had I previously. I cannot blame females any more than I can blame males. While fully aware of the responsibility that societal, religious, and practical considerations pertain to such cases, I give myself a pass by blaming nature and lack of wisdom.

I revolted within. I had paid and had been paying a considerable price with the first and last engagement with Olympia. I was not going to go through that again. I told Maria a solution had to be found as I was not getting involved if I could help it. Besides, I had my doubts about who the father might have been.

A religious family took her in at the recommendation of a Sacramento Greek gynecologist. She was treated regally. She had a good pregnancy and gave birth to a healthy boy. The doctor made arrangements for the adoption. Maria and I left the area and lost track of each other. Decades later, while visiting mutual friends in California, I learned that Maria had married a Florida realtor and was very unhappy. She died of cancer in her early sixties.

Toni

With Katerina long gone, Jeannie beatifically genuflecting on some parish pews, and Maria settled away, the field was now open for another female. Being very busy with my studies and night work, I was not looking. But somebody else was.

"May I sit next to you?" I heard the amiable voice of a beautiful 18-year-old female in one of my French Literature classes. Right away, my mind went automatic. I was flattered and momentarily beclouded. What did this lovely young lady find in me? The usual internal tremor possessed me, and I doubt I got much out of that class that day. My reaction was nothing new. Women always fascinated me and engendered a considerable reaction to my maleness. Instinct would take over, wisdom would take a back seat, and predictable vulnerability would enthrone itself firmly in the center. I would enter what I have labeled as my idiot mode.

Being in a good relationship with a member of the opposite sex offers some protection against further entanglements, but I had none then. I was easy prey. Still, given my lack of time and solid educational orientation, I pushed my usual thoughts aside and went about my business.

Some days later, as I was searching for a book in the library stacks, I saw that pretty face from my classroom smiling at me from the opposite side of a stack -- the devil at work. I smiled back, continued searching for my book, and rushed to my next class.

Sometime later, I was sitting at a large table in the library's open space, making notes from a book. When I took my eyes off the page, the guise of a familiar face demolished my concentration. This could not be accidental, I told myself. It was that same 18-year-old from the French class. Was she stalking me?

Her charming smile exposed two rows of perfectly shaped white teeth with only a partial retainer marring the beautiful landscape. This chrysalis left no doubt – she was interested in me. No, she was out to get me, would be more correct.

We all move by instinct at times. Sometimes, it works out; other times, it does not. That is how life is.

At any rate, my "idiot" mode kicked in, and I invited her for a cup of coffee. She informed me that she had participated in the orientation meeting I had led at the beginning of the semester. She liked my presentation and was pleased to have me as a classmate.

Still in idiot mode, I invited her to sit on the beautifully mowed grass in front of the library – it was a gorgeous spring day. I expounded on my grandiose plans for the future. She listened very attentively, not saying a word.

We spent the next 43 years together.

5. Return to Greece

Red carpet rollout

In the summer of 1963, I felt the time had come to visit Greece. Four years had elapsed since my departure. I had pined for my little daughter and had decided to bring her to America with me. My American partner had agreed to welcome my Greek daughter into our family. I do not know whether I missed my folks or my homeland. America suited me just fine. But there was an undeniable desire to return to Greece for a brief visit.

As I write this, I think that there was an element of unkindness in my decision to take my daughter to America. My folks had been raising her for four years. She had become the proverbial apple of their eye; she was a darling family member, the joy of their declining years.

What else was there to do? I could not just leave her in Greece! My life was in America, and she was my beloved little daughter. My parents swallowed the pill of separation with great difficulty and were great sports. They accepted their grief and offered little resistance, however painful that might have been. Collecting my child was a no-brainer for me, and in my youthful selfishness, I must have given it little thought. However, it does occur to me that I was somewhat blind to their pain. Re-reading letters written more than a half-century ago makes that point clear. Nor was it the best for the child. After all, my parents were the family she had known all her formative years.

I wish there had been a way to do things differently, but life without regrets does not exist.

The summer of 1963 was well into its course when I got on the plane for Greece. I had just finished an intensive study of the Russian language at the University of Washington right after completing my B.A. degree in Sacramento. I was bound for Greece. I had been away for four years and was looking forward to returning to see my folks and my little daughter. The last time I saw her was when I left in 1959. She was an infant then.

Seeing my folks after four years was as good as it could be. I cannot say I missed them, as they had tossed me out, and I had been living separately before leaving for America. Deep, hard feelings remained in my bruised soul. However, they were delighted to see me. They were genuinely proud of me. I had made them proud. In the narrow circle of the community's invasive eyes, my older sister's mental problems had lowered the family status considerably. Against that background, my academic successes were just the perfect antidote. My father could go to the community café, play cards with his friends, enjoy his ouzo, and bask in inflating his ego thanks to my accomplishments. I am told he wore my academic achievements as a badge of distinction. It had become his personal identification.

There was a time I became aware of it when I made a self-disparaging remark. "Oh, no! You cannot say that," my father protested as he held me in the highest possible esteem. His own self-esteem depended on my worthiness. I was glad to oblige.

Ironically, my father, of all people, had no right to derive any bragging rights from my academic achievements. After all, he had done a lot to hold me back from receiving a higher education and had broken his promises to support my university study in Italy twice.

Lost moped

When I left Greece for the first time to go to the US, I entrusted my moped to my brother. It was my most valuable investment. Four years later, when I returned to Greece after completing my B.A., I expected to find my bike dusty and somewhat rusty, to be sure. I looked for it in the barn behind the hotel where my brother and I had placed it. As it was not there, I asked my brother.

"I couldn't find the moped," I said.

"Oh, I got rid of it; it was broken up and didn't work anyway. It was worthless." He responded matter-of-factly. Now, I knew perfectly well it was in good condition when I left it with him. I was disappointed, but what could I do? I understand this is not the way I would have handled it myself. That bike had value, and I had kept it in good shape.

My brother's attitude bothered me, and I did not forget the incident. Years later, when he insisted on a second loan to remodel his hotel, I had no problem rejecting him. I did not have the enormous sum he demanded, and I knew he would never return a penny. The prevailing attitude was you do not borrow from an American – "they're all rich, money is lining the streets," -- you take it. He complained about my not "loaning" him the capital several times in later years. One time, I could not take it anymore. The injustice of the whole thing was boiling just below the surface inside me. I reminded my brother how he and Mother had thrown me out penniless into the streets and offered me nothing for SURVIVAL.

"Oh, you still remember that?" he said with a smirk. He had no idea of the damage he and Mother had caused me.

Many people, I have found, have low sensitivity to others' needs or viewpoints. They have difficulty empathizing and walking in another person's shoes. They only consider their own view, as if the other person has no side or does not exist. We call them egotists. At times, we even find ourselves in their midst. It would behoove one to remember that.

DEMETRIUS KOUBOURLIS PHD

6. Money Drain

M *oney to Olympia*
Olympia, my Greek spouse, and I kept our correspondence going. After all, we were husband and wife, bound by law. As the months passed and my parents took our little child in, Olympia could look at other life-changing opportunities.

Germany actively recruited many Turks, Greeks, and others to beef up its depleted post-war workforce. Olympia informed me she would like to emigrate to Germany. She would agree to give me the divorce if I paid for her fare to Germany and a bit more, something like 2000 dollars.

I did not have that money, as I was a financially strapped foreign student working nights and attending university in Sacramento. As much as I wanted to take her up on her offer, I could not. The deal went nowhere.

But the Fates were looking over me.

After completing my night shift with American Maintenance one night, I returned to my car, parked by the curbside near downtown Sacramento. I opened the door and readied to get in. At that instant, a truck drove by fast and struck my left door in its path, knocking it off its hinge and, fortunately, missing my left arm by what must have been a miraculous inch or so. The mangled door lay several feet in front of my car. The truck did not even slow down. I put together $1800 from my insurance and savings and sent it to Olympia after securing a written agreement for me to become the sole guardian of our daughter, Carletona.

My military obligation

After all arrangements were made and my folks said their tearful goodbyes to my daughter, we departed for Athens, where we would take the plane for the States the following day.

There was a glitch, however. The military would not let me leave. No exit visa for me! I was to be inducted into the Greek Air Force in three months.

No exit visa for you.
Military duty first.

A six-week battle with endless behind-the-doors machinations, testing the limits of available political pull, exhausting the kindness of a remote relative by overstaying my visit in Athens with my little daughter, draining my meager funds and begging, waiting and begging some more, going from public office to public office, fighting the exhausting bureaucracy, endlessly waiting for official translations of needed documents, and waiting some more to get more required documents from my American professors to be officially translated and be submitted and be delayed ad infinitum.

The whole system was designed with zero respect for the citizens. It felt like it was meant to humiliate, to keep enslaved and intimidated, baffled and overwhelmed, and constantly genuflecting before a mighty bureaucratic web.

In America, the attitude, as I have come to experience it, is that the bureaucracy is expected to serve the people. In Greece, at that time, it was close to the other way around. There was no respect or concept of the citizens' rights. It was a system of asking favors through one's connections to those in power. My family's political clout was zero, given that their party was out of rule, so I had to depend on some well-disposed remote relatives of my father's.

With great difficulty, I was finally granted a one-year deferment and was allowed to leave Greece.

∞∞∞∞

The agony of the experience is still with me. What a miserable situation! There seemed to be a continued concerted conspiracy against my education. What a painful waste of money and meager resources. I remember *swearing never to return* to my motherland. A feeling of profound disgust filled my soul. Why did such a mentality prevail in a once-enlightened land that became one of the world's best examples? Why did so many people go out of their way to put obstacles in other people's way and proceed as if this were normal? I came to feel this was a primitive state of affairs designed to keep the populace caged in. I wanted no part of it.

I marveled at the American mentality and sensed the freedom and independence of a respectful, law-abiding citizenry. In America, I felt the rules were the same for all. The system was set up to facilitate the citizens' affairs. It seemed everyone was for education; the universities were open to whoever, with or without formal qualifications. Prove you can do it, and you are in. This can-do spirit has filled me with enthusiasm, genuine respect, gratitude, and love for America and most of its institutions.

Yes, I am a great admirer of America. I am not ashamed, as some are, to proclaim my admiration. And not only. Far from attempting to project an image of nationalistic advocacy, I simply miss no opportunity to express my gratitude. America has satisfied all my dreams and more. It has been an open-ended welcomer of whatever I wished to accomplish. I have not encountered any institutionalized whimsicality of the kind reigning in Greece. Instead, just follow the rules, James! They are the same for all, no matter who your uncle is.

This is not to say that an ideal situation exists in America or that there is no favoritism. It is not as simple as that, as discrimination, for example, is in the same mix. Doors are not equally open to all. Let's face it.

What I have in mind when I deplore the Greek setup of my time with what I experienced in America is that there is simply no comparison. There were no fair chances in Greece, but I found more than that in America. Despite its shortcomings, America cannot be the baby you toss out with the bathwater. America has profound value.

∞∞∞∞

I could not return to Greece for years for fear of being inducted into the armed forces. My mother and brother had to go to Athens, visiting military authorities, with or without political support, to beg for another deferment. They had found a different reason to deny me another year's extension. I had not obtained my Master's degree after one year of graduate study. The notion that a master's degree takes only one year was indelibly inscribed in the mind of the military authority. However, I had not gotten the Master's for a different reason, to be explained later. Thus, my request for a second deferment extension was denied. I was given three months to report for service, after which I would be declared AWOL if I did not show up. By some kind of miracle, and thanks to the supportive letters of my graduate school professors, one of my relatives persuaded the authorities to grant me another year's extension.

I continued my graduate coursework and finished it in record time. I was given teaching assignments and decided not to return to oppressive Greece; I was going to become a citizen of a better country.

There was another problem, however. The Vietnam War was raging, and the possibility of getting nabbed was something else to consider. My Greek family informed me that after a lengthy consultation, they had decided the time had come for me to bring my family to Greece, to leave America.

What?

Do you see why I do not like wars and armies, although I recognize the necessity of protective and disciplinary authority under certain circumstances? Do you see why putting energy and resources into World Peace is worthwhile?

Laws change with time as new needs or insights evolve. So, paying my way out of military service finally became possible. The amount was significant; eventually, after four years, I could free myself from this nightmare. Greece's claws on me were loosening their grip. I could now return to the accidental motherland without fear of losing my freedom. And in time, I would not even want to return.

Support for parents

With age, my father followed the custom; he turned the business over to my brother for a nominal 5,000-drachma monthly payment, or about 165 dollars monthly at that time. However, the deal was not always adhered to. My parents asked me for financial assistance and never stopped asking, something my brother himself had warned me about years earlier.

To the extent I could, I helped, never forgetting their steadfast refusal and broken promises to support me when the tables were turned. *But I never said anything to them about that.* What for? Nothing was to be gained, and I chose the high road. I am glad I did.

When I recall examples of occasional meanness that I was the perpetrator of, I shudder to realize it did not matter in the long run and that it is too late to do anything about it now when only regrets remain.

Taking the high road has long-term dividends.

Dowry -- the major hindrance

No matter my argument, the dowry issue never ceased to bear its sharp teeth, barring my path. The Greek dowry custom goes back to ancient Greece. It will not surprise me if you think it goes back to Roman times, or it was widely practiced in Europe during the

Middle Ages, or it was an Ottoman Empire occupation left over, or it's still a significant problem in India only.

Dowries in Greece were, and may still be in some parts, material things like jewelry, money, linen, items to set up a household, and even real estate. It is what the bride contributes to the bridegroom. It is an unfair tradition with severe consequences. It has contributed to much suffering for my family and has been a bane, a blight, and a curse in my early life. It has done me serious harm.

"We must marry off your sisters before you can do your university studies," my father kept repeating his mantra. In the cultural environment, whether my sisters' dowries were more important than my education was a non-starter. The social pressure was unsurpassable. Conformity or shame, stigma, and embarrassment were the consequences. What was necessary for the rest of the family was a significant obstacle for me. Understanding this point mitigated my criticism somewhat, but not entirely. I get that now. My father had no intention of paying for my education. It was not on his list of priorities as it was not our society's priority, but marrying off his two daughters was.

∞∞∞

Over the years, my older sister Koula, coming of age, was a happy child who enjoyed singing traditional songs with her remarkable voice. Her unusual beauty could not fail but be noticed. Also, my family's higher-than-average financial position significantly improved the chances of a desirable match-up. Our little hotel cum restaurant provided a decent exposure platform – she was excellent marriage material. She was a great catch; my father knew he had superb merchandise.

And that was the problem.

Over several years, marriage proposals came but were rejected by my father.

"I'll marry her to a prince," he would say.

Meanwhile, the bazaar of the match-making process continued. My mother wasted no time finding defects in the proposed bridegrooms – they were not tall, good-looking, or young enough. One very insistent prospect, a greengrocer, was found undesirable because, although he was tall and well-to-do enough, he reportedly spat on the hotel floor while spending the night there. Another candidate even asked me to intercede with my father. The answer was always negative. My parents were waiting for their prince to show up.

A diabolical event made my path to higher education even more impassable.

∞∞∞∞

Our establishment was located across from the railroad tracks. An additional track facilitated the stopover of a train to allow another train from the opposite direction to go by or to be used for unloading delivered materials. As most railroad functions in those days were manual, a station master was necessary. At this time, the state-owned organization responsible for running the railroad network had built a structure consisting of offices and living quarters right by the side of the tracks.

A remote relative of my mother's was hired to replace the station master, who had recently passed away. The new station master was young, good-looking, and available. Although he developed an intimate relationship with the beautiful young widow of the deceased railroad master, his visits to our family or his strutting back and forth from the station to the manual track lever exchange caught the attention of my older sister from across the tracks. In short, my sister fell in love with him. This was a disaster.

What followed was a series of severe reprimands from my father. I'm not privy to details, but my beautiful sister soon began behaving strangely. For instance, while conversing with someone, she would turn her head and stare at her right side. This got worse. She became a family embarrassment. My parents were distraught. What to do?

The best advice they secured was to take her to an Athens clinic. It was a private, expensive establishment that dealt with mental diseases and reportedly did lobotomies. The now-discredited lobotomies were popular in Greece in the '40s and '50s. Psychiatrists and neurosurgeons performed them routinely. Although I have no direct knowledge of this, I suspect a lobotomy was performed on my sister. A lobotomy involves surgically severing neural connections in the brain's pre-frontal cortex.

My sister spent several months in the clinic. When she finally returned home, she was a changed person. Gone were her angelic beauty and her carefree singing. She had to take prescribed pills daily. For life! She began gaining weight.

My father's prime marriage merchandise was spoiling.

Rumors about my "crazy" sister began spreading in the community. Marriage prospects disappeared. She became a persona to avoid. My family became one to avoid. My younger sister's prospects also became seriously affected. My family's desperate efforts to protect the family's reputation were ineffective. No one wanted to marry my beautiful, gifted sister, and my younger sister would be of marrying age soon.

And I was supposed to put my education on hold until my sisters married! Who are you kidding, Father? Mother? Siblings?

∞∞∞∞∞

The dowry then was an obstacle and a burden for the whole family, including me. The dowry's tentacles held onto me tightly. It did not matter that my father had deceived me twice, that the family had thrown me cruelly into the streets and did not provide any financial support for me. It did not matter that I had been on my own for many years; it did not matter that I had my own family and had been living and studying in the United States.

The dowry matter rose its ugly head once more. I was a poor graduate student at the University of Washington, barely making ends meet, when my father wrote *demanding* that I contribute one-third toward my younger sister's dowry. I could have ignored his demand. I could have said I was an impoverished graduate student without his support, which was true. I could have said that, as you did not help me with my education, I cannot see how I can help you with the dowry. Instead, I chose to participate when I could least afford it. My father's moral hold and the society I grew up in were so powerful, even after many years away from the paternal family.

I went to a bank and applied for a loan. I was asked to provide a financial report. The loan was denied. Then, I went back later and emptied my heart on the lap of the sympathetic bank loan officer. He asked me to come back in a few days.

A loan for $3000 US dollars was granted with a low interest rate. It took me a long time to repay, but I did. This was when I was a graduate student with a wife and a child in kindergarten. At that time, as we could not afford heat, we huddled in one bed at night to keep warm.

∞∞∞

My younger sister, Chrisanthi, had to be ingenious and resourceful to get married and leave my father's aegis. She had to "earn" her freedom from my father's clutches and set up her own family. She related her own tale of woe to me with passionate fervor.

The "spice of life" is sometimes just that, as with Chrisanthi. A spice peddler would come by Rion about once a week. His whole store was on a bicycle. He would open his triptych of a display showing various spice samples, a larger quantity of which he carried on the bike's side bags. He could also take orders for whatever was wanted. He was a very orderly fellow. Over the years of selling spices to my family, he came to know Chrisanthi as an intelligent, proper, hard-working young lady, and it occurred to him that she would make a great wife for one of his relatives. He broached the subject with my parents, and although they were amenable, there were problems with the dowry amount. Neither my sister nor her intended had met each other. The financial details of the dowry had to be settled first. The future bridegroom, a heavy equipment operator, and his family wanted much more money than my father was willing to part with.

My parents must have had the money, but the major part was destined for my older sister. (My mother had been saving Great Britain Gold Sovereign coins in the tubular frame of her bed.)

Chrisanthi knew the score and wanted to get married in the worst way. My parents' dilly-dallying was not helping. They were taking too long with their negotiations. My sister and her future husband met and liked each other immediately. They wanted to make the marriage a reality in the worst way possible. This is what my father could take advantage of and did. My father was always on the lookout for quality free labor. He exploited me without remuneration and was doing so with my siblings.

Why not add another free hand to the mix?

It was so that Polis, my sister's future husband, came to work for my father to earn part of the agreed dowry. He helped with the restaurant after his regular work for some time. Chrisanthi continued working to achieve the agreed dowry amount. As I was not part of the family then, all the info I have is from letters, which I still possess.

∞∞∞∞

One would have no issue with declaring my father exploitative. But one comes up empty-handed when trying to figure out how I could have behaved so incomprehensibly, to deprive my family and myself of what we could not afford to accede to my father's wishes. One would be justified to call my sacrifice idiotic. Why did I let my father again and again exploit me? What kind of moral hold did he have over me?

A possible explanation mentioned earlier comes to mind nowadays: I was brainwashed. My family and the culture were the enduring formative forces in my milieu, and I was a carrier of my Greek culture. Certain things were not questioned. It was the law of the land. And I wanted to be a good son, approved of and maybe loved a little bit.

Culture has a long reach. Never underestimate the cultural hold on any country's denizens. Whether we realize it or not, the traditions we were raised with become a part of who we are. Some customs give us pleasure and comfort; some enslave and victimize us. Culture, as a guiding force, exerts a powerful influence on us, determining our beliefs and how we interact. A culture's social norms, whether verbal or non-verbal or explicitly prescribed, can force us to fall in line or be stigmatized.

To the comfort of my father's memory, I have concluded that I was not the dowry's only victim in my family; we all were: my siblings, mother, and even my father! Culture does not merely have a hold on us; it has a stranglehold!

DEMETRIUS KOUBOURLIS PHD

7. Graduate studies

My UW teachers
While completing my B.A. degree at Sacramento State College (now the University of California at Sacramento), I applied to half a dozen universities for graduate study. Acceptance letters came from all of them. I chose the University of Washington. I was admitted to the graduate program of the Slavic and East European Languages and Literatures Department.

I would be remiss if I failed to extol my good teachers at the University of Washington's Slavic Department. From the beginning, I was embraced as a member of their intellectual family. From the first intensive Russian Language and Literature courses, teachers from Russia, Hungary, the United States, Czechoslovakia, Bulgaria, and Israel showered me with interest and attention. They treated me respectfully; some even took me aside and offered unsolicited encouragement and advice.

"Chekhov would be proud of your Russian," my intensive Russian Language teacher once said.

However, what must have set me apart from my fellow students was one daring thing I did. I wrote my first Russian Literature paper in French instead of English.

"Что пришло вам в голову?" (What got into your head?) exclaimed my befuddled teacher after he had read the paper. Yeah, really, what had gotten into my head? For one, the higher-class Russians of his and some preceding generations spoke in French and reserved Russian only when dealing with the peasantry. For another, I wanted to show off. The department buzzed with the news: "A Greek student wrote his Russian Literature paper in French." Then later, "The Greek student wrote his paper in French." And then, "Demetrius wrote his paper in French." I had arrived at the department.

Another Russian teacher, Mr. Gribanovski, an elegant man of exemplary manners, clearly of a higher class, singled me out. He wanted to chat with me in French, either to find out how the department's Greek spoke French or to show me that he knew the language well himself. In brief, my crazy idea of writing in French had a dramatic effect on the department. My status was established. I was lifted one rung.

A professor from Hungary, Imre Boba, proved as unpretentious and helpful as possible. He made sure I had a good background in Russian history. Besides teaching East European history, he was responsible for the university library's East European collection. Sanskrit was not one of his languages, but neither was it mine. He persuaded me to transcribe Devanagari script book titles for his library work. The only problem was that I had to learn a complex script just for that job. I forgot it soon afterward.

My Russian Literature professor, Dr. Jurij Ivask, a gentle and gentlemanly soul who had left Russia before it became the Soviet Union, treated me with unusual respect. He gave me several Russian books and would ask me to read out loud poems by Constantine Cavafy and Giorgos Seferis in Greek. These Greek poets had both received the Nobel Prize for Literature. As he did not know Greek, I wondered what attracted him to the sound of Greek poetry.

It will be recalled that after completing my B.A. in 1963, I returned to Greece to fetch my little daughter, who had lived with my parents for about four years. However, the Greek military would not allow me to return to the US to continue my studies – they wanted to draft me. My University of Washington teachers wasted no time composing letters of support for me to be allowed to continue my studies.

These good people played a significant role in honing my education and guiding me toward specialization within the Slavic field.

One of my teachers, a lady from Israel, took me aside after class: "With your background in languages, you belong in linguistics. Go see Dr. Abernathy." Which I did.

"What took you so long?" he asked. Evidently, someone must have mentioned me to him. Thus, I became his student, and he became my major professor.

∞∞∞∞

Dr. Robert Abernathy specialized in Slavic Linguistics when not writing science fiction stories. Generally regarded as a Harvard prodigy and revered like no other in the department, he went out of his way to salvage my hurt feelings, which his severe criticism of my first paper in his class had engendered. Unbeknownst to me, an author referenced in my paper happened to be one of my professor's least favorite scholars.

An aloof and mostly reserved man, this good professor did something that did not come easy for him. When my hurt feelings kept me away from his classes for a few days, he sent a delegation of classmates to persuade me to return. And return, I did. Several months later, he invited me into his office and pronounced unforgettable words.

"You're Ph.D. material. You don't need the MA. You're going straight for the Ph.D."

"Really, really???" I asked, not believing my ears.

"I don't make it a habit of telling such to my students," was my professor's dry reply, approaching annoyance.

I distinctly recall his semi-reclined position, right hand close to his mouth, holding a lit cigarette, elbow resting on his chair, and legs crossed. This was one of his peculiar thinking poses. When he was not doing that or leafing through a book, he would have a cup of coffee in his right hand. An electric immersion water heater would lie within reach. A heavy smoker and coffee drinker, he indeed was.

Although standoffish with just about everyone, he showed me signs of preference and occasionally cracked a smile. I do not recall him using customary greetings like "good morning, " "goodbye, " etc. I suppose he regarded such words as superfluous and below his dignity. A man of few words, indeed. On the rare moments when he made what he considered a brilliant remark, he would conclude his controlled laughter with a deep air intake.

Professor Abernathy was a student of Roman Jacobson, the legendary Harvard Slavic Linguistics scholar, and knew Noam Chomsky well. I got to meet both Chomsky and Jacobsen, thanks to Dr. Abernathy. I still have one of his handwritten letters, in which he informs me that he had shown Jacobson a preliminary draft of my dissertation and that Jacobson had expressed interest in publishing it upon completion.

∞∞∞∞

The Department of Slavic and East European Languages and Literatures offered various specializations in the Slavic field. Having been recommended for the highest degree without needing an M.A. saved much time. To my knowledge, I was the only one of Dr. Abernathy's students to get that valuable pass-through. Without that, it would have taken longer to fulfill my Ph.D. requirements. I completed the designated courses in record time -- two and a half years! To add German and Italian to my official dossier, I took qualifying tests administered by the University of Washington. As a graduate student, I spent all my time studying, including the summers. During the last summer of my coursework, I was assigned to teach the intensive Russian language grammar course for all language sections.

∞∞∞∞

One summer, the idea came to teach a brief spoken Modern Greek course. The book and film *Zorba, The Greek* by Nikos Kazantzakis, and the music by Mikis Theodorakis, the great composer, were at their height. Everyone fancied a bit of Zorba in themselves and became enamored with the *Sirtaki,* Zorba's dance.

Quixotic Zorba's devil-may-care philosophy was catchy, and the music, now mainstream, was divine. All my teachers, without exception, took part in that brief course.

No, we did not practice the *Sirtaki*.

It was a strange feeling to reverse roles for a while. We had fun lunching together in a classroom and drilling common Greek words and expressions.

Some years later, I returned to the department and relished sharing some bottles of exquisite seven-star Metaxa brandy my father had brought to the U.S. for resale.

∞∞∞∞

What did my teachers in America teach me? More than anything, my undergraduate and graduate teachers showed me genuine interest and caring. I felt somehow unique. My teachers in America had a different mentality from my Greek teachers. Culture played a role here. Greek teachers lacked the notion of closeness with their students. A cultivated distance was the norm. There was a barrier, one of position with authoritative and high-handed status, which my American teachers did not fancy. My American teachers were much more approachable and involved. They were less authoritative and more humane. I sensed that and delighted in the difference. I often think of how inadequate my appreciation of my teachers was. Only as time passed did I understand how good these human beings were and how lucky I was to have been their student.

My Generals

At ease! This has nothing to do with the Greek army.

When all the required coursework was completed, the time came for the General Ph.D. Exams or the Generals. The candidate was required to submit to a department-wide examination. Select department members and specialists in the areas of the candidate's field formed part of the Generals committee. A rigorous multi-hour examination took place for any committee member to ask the candidate questions. At the end of the procedure, the candidate was asked to step outside and await the committee's deliberations for as long as the committee needed to agree to a pass or fail.

I do not remember how long I waited for the committee's door to open, but it seemed like what an ancient Greek *eon* might have been. When the door finally opened, my heart began beating unusually fast. My principal professor, Dr. Robert Abernathy, asked me to enter the conference room. I tried to make some sense of his poker face, but it was in vain.

I crossed the threshold like a dog, tail tucked tightly behind, uncertain of its immediate fate. I took a quick reading of all the faces around the table. They were waiting politely for Dr. Abernathy to speak. He made some introductory remarks – Where is he going with this? I wondered -- fearing the worst. His usually delayed conversational mode strained my heart. For a moment, I thought he was trying to make nice, to cushion the blow.

"Congratulations, Demetrius!" he finally uttered, exhibiting some satisfaction and pride because one of his students had made it this far.

This was a central station on the way to the much-coveted Ph.D. Many candidates fail and are returned to additional coursework, or it is indirectly suggested that they forget it. Some get discouraged and give up. But getting passed, especially the first time, meant a great deal. I had made it thus far with flying colors. I was filled with indescribable joy.

As soon as all the other members congratulated me, I rocketed out of the conference room. I sprinted home non-stop. I had never covered the distance so fast before. I was turbocharged. I remember my heart pounding fast and my lungs in great need of air. But I kept running. I had to share the news with my little family. This was crucial news for us. It was the culmination of a protracted, dedicated effort. It was part of that larger struggle to complete my formal education.

Dissertation jitters

Now, with my Generals behind me, I could begin to work on my thesis. A thesis, also known as a dissertation, is expected to be an original contribution to knowledge in the candidate's chosen field. The candidate, or occasionally the major professor, proposes a topic, and the real work begins.

One must read many books about the chosen topic, ripen, and write. Work is presented to the principal professor, suggestions are made, and a long dialog develops, which can last for years and occasionally never ends. Drafts get submitted and rejected till "perfection" is achieved.

∞∞∞∞

Dr. Abernathy's replacement at the University of Washington was Dr. Lew Reed Mickleson, an extraordinarily amiable and hard-working individual. This was a pleasant contrast to the habitually reserved Dr. Abernathy. One was extroverted, the other a clear introvert.

As my thesis topic, I proposed investigating the Russian verbal aspect, a thorny area in the language. Aspect is how languages look at an action, which differs from time. Aspect tells us whether the action is ongoing or completed. For a simplified example of what aspect is in English, consider "he was eating" versus "he ate," continuous versus non-continuous (other terms exist). Both examples here are in the past tense, but one is ongoing, and the other is not. The difference is aspect.

"Corpus" describes the material linguists use to conduct their research. I chose the VOA (Voice of America) Russian language broadcasts as my corpus to investigate the Russian verbal aspect. I used statistics as my method. My dissertation's title is *A Statistical Investigation of the Russian Verbal Aspect,* University of Washington, 1967.

Listening to VOA broadcasts with short-wave radios proved somewhat challenging for a non-native of the Russian language with the iffy technology of the time. Still, I was able to gather sufficient material for my corpus requirements to conduct my study.

Felicitously, graduate studies were not the only yield from my graduate school years. I was to be graced with something else, which has become even more important in my life.

A hidden treasure

There was a time when no one talked about it, at least not in my circles. I do not know if it was taboo, but I never heard about it during my B.A. years in Sacramento or post-graduate studies in Seattle. I was unaware of any mention of it, oral or written, in my reading adventures. It could be it was totally accidental. But I knew beyond any doubt that I had found a real treasure.

A hidden treasure.

Hidden among the hundreds of dusty paperback volumes of a favorite used bookstore at the Seattle University District, I found a small book, *Yoga and Health*, by Selvarayan Yesudian and Elizabeth Haich, Harper and Row 1953. A thorough perusal of its table of contents led to my reading of the Prologue, which loosened my super-tight graduate student purse strings -- twenty-five cents, all the way down from its new copy price of seventy-five cents.

I figured I could afford it.

It turned out to be the most essential book acquisition of my life. My more than 16 years of schooling up until then had not taught me what was contained in this little book.

It was a blueprint for a healthier life.

After acquainting myself with the contents, I followed the suggested exercise regime. Thankfully, I was blessed with patience, determination, and perseverance and could teach myself how to do the exercises and what each one was supposed to do for me.

This is what I had been looking for.

Experiencing firsthand the immediate results made me a faithful practitioner. I turned away from the traditional philosophy of medications, however beneficial they can be at times. I became a self-curer. I specialized in my "patient-cure-thyself" philosophy. I established a life-long conversation with myself. And I found my cures to be adequate equipment for a healthy, disease-free, clear-minded life.

What more could one want?

I want to clarify that I'm not suggesting that the reader follow my example; I'm simply reporting on my experience. Your doctor is a proper source of medical advice.

∞∞∞∞

There came a time when my casual mention of yoga met with opprobrium and unambiguous disapproval akin to pseudo-intellectual better-than-thou ridicule. I got the hint and was determined to keep it under wraps. It did not matter that my cohorts were scornful and even censorial. I decided mine was not to proselytize but to go about my business.

Years later, yoga began entering the mainstream. Yoga schools sprouted all over, albeit gradually. A strange feeling invades me when some enthusiastic soul mentions yoga in my presence. "What took you so long, world?" my inner voice pipes up. What was a scorned, unhidden treasure in my youth is now commonplace. Better late than never! I often wonder why such an important issue was not central to my education. Why had untold hours been devoted to studying many exciting and valuable things but not yoga?

With the help of yoga, I could follow and am still pursuing a healthy and productive life. The quality of my life is owed to yoga. People familiar with my chronological age frequently approach me, wanting to know my secret.

"Yoga," I respond laconically as if by habit.

And here's a pictorial postscript intending to inspire: My father died at age 80, my mother at 75, an older sister at 70, and here I am at 86:

This is an unretouched picture of the peacock posture (mayurasana), an advanced pose reserved for yoga adepts.

Thank you, yoga!

DEMETRIUS KOUBOURLIS PHD

8. Academic ladder

*A**ssistant Professor*
Once my Ph.D. coursework was completed, the time had come to leave my nest and try my wings at some professorial job. I was expected to look for a teaching position. And so it was when Dr. Robert Abernathy, my principal professor at the University of Washington, accepted a senior post with the Department of Slavic Languages and Literatures at the University of Colorado at Boulder that he also secured a job for me there. This was my first job outside the University of Washington, where I had fulfilled my Ph.D. requirements. I was entering a professorial career.

Going with my principal professor was thought to speed up the writing of my Ph.D. dissertation. In any event, I felt honored, flattered, and grateful that my professor procured a job for me at his new place of employment. The appointment was a welcome surprise, and I remain thankful.

I was assigned a full teaching load of Russian language courses at the University of Colorado. I was also asked to teach an evening class at the University of Colorado's Denver Center in Denver. The teaching load was heavy, and it became unbearably heavier when a department member was killed in an auto accident. I was asked to add all his courses to my own load -- they were all advanced Slavic Linguistics material! I found myself having little time for dissertation research. I did the best I could but was not exactly happy. I worked off my tension many days in Boulder, jogging up to the Flat Iron Mountains and running down zealously. Running at that altitude seemed more effortless, or was it the magic air?

So, when a tempting job offer came from the renowned Tulane University with a very light teaching load and more money, I decided to take it.

The Dissertation

While teaching as an Assistant Professor at Tulane University, with a relatively light teaching load, I could devote much time to researching and writing my dissertation. I was fortunate to have Dr. Mickleson take over as my dissertation advisor at the University of Washington. He was excited about my topic and wasted no time responding to my drafts by return mail. He was responsive in every sense of the term. He wasted no time mailing his corrections and suggestions to my drafts by return mail. I will remain grateful to him for the rest of my life.

My preferred working method was to visit the famed Tulane Football Stadium, a vast football field, always open and completely empty when not used for games. It was within walking distance of the faculty housing where we stayed. It is in this stadium that I wrote my dissertation.

A clipboard and a pen were my weapons of choice. I would leave my writing tools on a bleacher and jog around the football field while working on dissertation issues in my mind. Upon returning to the starting point where my writing tools were, I would jot down the results of my accelerated peripatetic method. When returning home later, I would clean things up, and my wife, a champion typist, would type up clean copies and mail them immediately to Dr. Mickleson in Seattle. While waiting for his corrections and suggestions, I would continue with the available material. No time was wasted.

The creative process also benefited from a systematic use of my subconscious. I would take the thorny issue of the day to bed with me. Without fail, my reliable subconscious would deliver the results the following day. It was a happy coupling of my circadian entities. The dissertation was "squeezed out" of my head in about three months.

Dr. Mickleson never failed to send me his corrections by return mail. Once, he expressed an unforgettable compliment: "You're the cleverest fellow I've ever known."

Doesn't praise feel good?

Yeah, so long as you do not let it get into your head, it is wisely said.

The Ph.D.

When all thought matures, resulting in an acceptable original contribution to knowledge, your thesis director presents the final version to a special committee. The candidates must confront a formidable Ph.D. committee and be prepared to answer any questions its members may ask. The members of this committee are typically professors from various departments, not just the candidate's department. So, surprises are quite possible. The department dean generally decides who will participate in a candidate's committee. Universities safeguard their reputation by ensuring that granted Ph. D.s meet exceedingly high standards.

Ph.D. stands for Doctor of Philosophy, an abbreviation of the Latin term (Ph)ilosophiae (D)octor. A doctor is a learned person, a teacher. The Ph.D. tradition started in the 12th century, aiming to recognize and foster advanced knowledge and expertise.

With my dissertation accepted by the University of Washington's Slavic Languages and Literatures Department, the time came for its defense. The prospect of defending a dissertation raises chilling goosebumps in the hearts of a Ph.D. candidate. It is a distressing initiation rite. The thought alone spreads dread, and it was no different with me.

At the appointed time, in the fall of 1967, I flew from New Orleans to Seattle to defend my dissertation.

Much of what we go through in life is a battle of nerves. We need to have ways at our disposal to fortify whatever is required to get the job done. My tenacity came from a long-established conversation with myself. Full of confidence, with my inner turbulence under strict control, I entered the committee's fearsome atmosphere. I managed to answer all questions with ease. After all, I was the foremost expert on my chosen subject then. I had to be. I had to contend with some pirouetting egos, whose aim seemed more to impress with their own knowledge than to ascertain mine.

I was called back in after the customary wait-outside-the-conference-room procedure to allow the committee members to debate my performance.

"Demetrius," my dissertation professor began as if to clear his throat, "Dr. Koubourlis," he triumphantly announced, and after a brief pause, he added, "Congratulations." This seemed pleonastic, redundant, as the "Dr." had already informed me of my success.

Being called "Dr." for the first time had the ring of a bell of delicious joy most mortals will never hear, no matter how much money they have -- tell that to those super-rich who compete with each other via the length of their yachts. A doctorate is the recognition of your peers and the admission to their ethereal club for life. In my case, it was the coveted reward of a long struggle, a veritable battle, to reach the pantheon of American education.

I was granted a Ph.D. in the fall of 1967. According to the U.S. Census Bureau, only 1.2% of Americans hold a Ph.D. degree!

Thank you, America, for allowing me to enter your venerable halls of intellectual achievement!

It took me eight years from first coming to the United States to obtain my B.A. and Ph.D. degrees. This is regarded as unusually fast by typical standards. However, I worked hard and showed unwavering dedication, and my dream of acquiring the highest degree from an American university became a reality.

∞∞∞∞

While teaching at Tulane, I presented some of my work at a scholarly conference at the University of Florida in Tallahassee. I was immediately offered an excellent job at the University of North Carolina at Chapel Hill (UNC). I taught various courses there, including Russian Language and Comparative Slavic Linguistics for the Slavic department. I guest-taught a course in Mathematical Linguistics for the Linguistics department and a course on Computer Programming for the Humanities for the Computer Science Department for three consecutive years. This was heady stuff.

I also found time to go to the Soviet Union. In 1970, with a group of my UNC students, I joined more U.S. professors and their students for a study and travel summer session at Djuny in Leningrad.

However, some problems developed with the new chairman of the Slavic department at UNC, who was none other than the one who had hired me at the University of Colorado two years earlier. With my help, he became the chairman of the Slavic department at UNC but proved ungrateful. He wanted to change my courses and advocated my directing the doctoral work of a Mathematical Linguistics Ph.D. candidate. I did not feel I had the time and told him so. This led to fundamental disagreements and his recommendation to not renew my contract, which resulted in my leaving UNC after completing three very productive teaching and research years.

∞∞∞∞

Moscow, Idaho, was billed as the Garden of Eden, an idyllic place where Idaho's principal learning institution was. I was looking for a welcoming atmosphere and a light teaching load. Three hours, three days a week, amounted to nine work hours per week. This left a lot of time for research. I had already been working on several projects. The heavy teaching load at UNC did not allow much time for study and advancement.

The computer department at the University of Idaho received me with open arms. There were hardly any humanities professors using the giant IBM 360 at the time. The university was anxious to utilize this resource. Justifying the acquisition and maintenance expenses may have been among the reasons, as well as advancing research. I was even offered programming assistance. However, I had learned long before that programming needs and programming skills are best when joined in one mind. At the University of Washington, I discovered that cross-communication was a waste of time, and I taught myself what programming was needed for my research. I achieved my goal, published computer-assisted articles and books following that philosophy, and offered a programming course at UNC for three years.

I am grateful to the University of Idaho in the sincerest way for providing me practically unlimited support. At one time, I had 13 people doing transliteration work for my concordance projects; also, the computer department public relations officer accompanied me to Stanford to explore a joint computer-assisted project. Another time, the same officer came to my office, offering unlimited support for my research.

Then, in addition, the UI Research Foundation took me in. I was assigned a second office there and was encouraged to submit a university-wide grant application to NEH, the National Endowment for the Humanities, to research Euthanasia. I even went to Washington, DC, to lobby for support. I met with Idaho's senatorial and congressional Representatives and lobbied for their support. The publishing arm of the Idaho Research Foundation enabled me to establish a Language Series as the Editor, and in a very short time, we published two books. Then, more requests for publication came but had to be rejected due to capital restrictions.

My time at UI was the most productive in my career. The University President opened his inner circle to me thanks to the support of a vital administration friend. Alas, I was not cut out to be an administration functionary. I was at my happiest and most productive doing my scholarly research solo.

I also became an American citizen in 1972.

Associate Professor

A frenzy of publication activity was unfurled. First was my *Soviet Academy Grammar, a computer-aided Index (1972),* followed by my *A Concordance to the Poems of Osip Mandelstam* (Cornell University Press, 1974), *Topics in Slavic Phonology* (Slavica Press, 1974), and several scholarly articles.

My scholarly output at the University of Idaho was noted. But my rank was still Assistant Professor. The President's Office took notice, and I got promoted to Associate Professor.

Full Professor

The following year, I was promoted to Full Professor! I may have been the youngest full professor at the university. I was also granted the coveted tenure status. Indeed, the University of Idaho treated me well, and I re-confirm my gratitude.

I was then the only Full Professor in the Foreign Languages Department. Outranking all, including the chairman, meant I was deciding who got raises and promotions. Until then, my department colleagues had been rationalizing their thinking to keep me at the assistant level till hell froze over.

During my first year at the University of Idaho, I was subjected to a civil form of discrimination, cultured and polite. First, my department chairman moved my office away from the department to a different building across campus; yes, I would still be allowed to come over and have lunch in their august company, I was graciously reminded. Next, I was not invited to the social departmental get-togethers.

When I gained the rank advantage over all department members, including the chairman, do you think I would use my advantage to get even? Not in a million years! I am proud of myself for that. I went out of my way to be as objective and non-vengeful as possible because I consider "getting even" unworthy of the person I aspire to be. One may wonder whether my Christian upbringing had something to do with this. Perhaps. However, it exemplifies the nobility my soul yearned for. It aligns with my Socratic pursuit of moral excellence in my interminable efforts for a good and fulfilling life.

I was not going to play Count Monte Christo with my rank advantage. Period. I always thought that professors ought to be better people. They ought to be exemplars of our society. Unfortunately, becoming a classics scholar does not make one a better person unless one is confusing education with character. You take your person with you in whatever job role you play.

Years later, however, when I had distinguished myself in yet another field, the same colleagues invited me to dinner and placed me at the head of the long table, showing me unusual respect. It was evident my colleagues had done some good thinking.

∞∞∞∞

Although all was going well with teaching, research, and university-sponsored scholarly travel, something important was missing. My family was growing; I had bright children and dreamt of providing the best education for them. Besides their canonical schooling, they got exposed to music and dance lessons, as many children are. To enhance their education, I was able to borrow the audio-visual center's science slide collections and spent evenings reviewing them with my children and wife. There would be no problem for them to get tuition-free education as members of a UI professor.

Still, I had bigger plans for them.

DEMETRIUS KOUBOURLIS PHD

9. Tidying up my first family matters

ather's will

*F*There always comes a time when we must set our first family's file aside. It is never a clean operation. Our first family experiences never leave us but become increasingly distant with time, especially if physical separation is a factor. The passing of one's parents provides a definitive pivot. My parents were the glue that bound my siblings and me in some unique way. The bond weakened with time as other concerns took over – our own families, careers, and geographical distance. Money matters may have also accelerated the dilution of our parents' hearth. Let me disregard the strict chronological order of my life's trajectory to wrap up my father's family and its influence and effect on my siblings and me.

In the fall of 1982, my father, feeling moribund, phoned with an urgent request; he asked me to go to Greece to assist him with his will. He could have asked his wife and any child, who were right there, not 10,000 kilometers away. When I arrived, my father immediately took me aside and reminded me he had little time to live. He stated that I was the only child he could trust. He was apportioning his properties, giving me the lion's share.

"Δεν θελω τιποτα, πατερα, (I don't want anything, Father,)" I said, refusing his offer. There were reasons for my refusal. My siblings believed they had earned those properties themselves with their hard work, whereas I had not participated fully. Additionally, I had other personal, deeply indelible reasons.

Undeterred, my father endeavored again to persuade me to accept his offer the following day. I refused to budge.

"OK, then." He said resignedly. "I will leave half of the Antirrion property to John, your son. I know you wouldn't want to prevent that because I wish that property to remain in Koubourlian hands as it came from my mother."

Meanwhile, as my father and I sat outside at a small table at the family's original home, going through the inheritance deliberations, my brother and mother spied on us from across the road, whispering conspiratorially. It was not difficult to guess what they were thinking. If only they knew what I was doing for their sake!

My involvement consisted of steadfastly refusing any share in my father's assets. As for the property division among the others, I left it up to my father. But they did not know my role then, so one can forgive them for their suspicions.

∞∞∞∞

How does greed get depicted on a person's face? Where there is greed, there is no love. I took notice of those glances and conspiratorial looks over the few days my father and I worked out the details of his will. I consider all that a natural human reaction and bear no ill will. It didn't even occur to me that it was an excellent opportunity to get even with my mother and brother for banning me from the paternal home that fateful day in the fall of 1957.

Beware, what goes around comes around.

∞∞∞∞

While still figuring out the will matters, my father wanted to make one last trip to Antirrion, his birthplace, across the straights. He asked my brother and me to take him there. The pretext was the olive grove, his inheritance from his mother, which he was bequeathing to my brother's son and mine.

My brother came along reluctantly but could not hide his profound hatred for my father. As my father sat on the ground under an old olive tree to catch his breath, I took my brother aside and beseeched him to make his peace with our father as he was dying. A while later, I proposed we drive to Nafpaktos, to Gribovo, a few kilometers away, a favorite spot of old for lunch. My father liked the idea. My brother tagged along begrudgingly. We had a good lunch, which my father enjoyed, and I felt I was making progress.

∞∞∞∞

During those days, I could have revealed a family secret to my father, probably removing my brother's son from inheritance contention and benefiting my son. My brother's son was not his pre-marriage child with his wife, as my parents had been told. He had been adopted following my input and encouragement years earlier because my brother and his wife could not have children. To avoid the impression that my brother's lie had no significance, one needs to understand how important it was for my father to believe my brother's son was a true Koubourlis, a product of the same bloodline. But I kept the secret to myself.

∞∞∞∞

The following day, my father scheduled a meeting with a Patras notary. In Greece, as in other countries, a notary, not a lawyer, usually specializes in wills. I was presented with a copy of my father's will. Despite my protests, I noticed in the document that my father was still bequeathing most of his estate to me.

"I've told you I don't want anything," I exclaimed. I wanted to add some specific words overflowing from my soul. They had been struggling to burst out since he broke his promises to help me study, and I got tossed into the streets penniless to sink or swim. Persistently, those words would surface automatically, but I would suppress them. I did so this time as well. Still trying to persuade me, he said:

"Your brother will eat it all up," He meant my brother would sell it off and waste the money. There was not much to counter, as that was also my opinion.

"Think about it," he said, "I want the properties to remain in the family. This is my wish. I know I can trust you with that."

"Sorry, Father, I want no part of your properties." He could not understand why I refused to accept. Again, I suppressed those words, erupting from my most profound depths. I could see my father's disappointment and had no desire to aggravate a dying man's last days.

We returned to the notary the next day, and I was presented with the final copy. I read it carefully and noticed I was given 10,000 Greek drachmas, a nominal amount comparable to the notary's cost of putting the will together. Once more, I objected.

According to Greek law, the notary explained, something had to be given to each family member to ensure everyone was accounted for and that there would be no problems afterward.

I could not argue with that and let it go. The will obligated my brother to pay me the 10,000 drachmas my father was bequeathing me. I never got it. I did not get any money for the record, but I also paid for the will, which coincidentally was 10,000 drachmas!

When we returned to Father's house, I kept the details of the will to myself and left Greece the following day. I have no idea what my father told the family then or later, and it may be they learned about the will's contents only after his death.

Parents dying

When my father was terminally ill, he somehow believed I had the magic power to do something about it. I dropped everything and went to his bedside in Greece. All I could do was console him with my presence and ensure that some last-minute favors were extended, such as obtaining a particular mattress from Athens, convincing the doctor to allow him to smoke a cigarette, and, most importantly, fulfilling his wish to spend his final days at home with the doctor agreeing to visit regularly. His lung cancer had metastasized by the time I reached him.

∞∞∞∞∞

Less than two years later, my mother was bedridden in the same private clinic my father had been in. I was asked to rush to Greece to be at her side. She had some special wishes which I was able to satisfy. When I was kneeling by her bedside, she told me she had missed me all those years. This brought convulsive tears to my eyes.

The doctors did everything they could, but her advanced liver cancer was inoperable.

"Why kill her?" I was told, "She'll be dead in a few days anyway." An operation was thought unnecessary.

As relatives typically avoided telling a patient of the seriousness of their ailment, my mother suspected her illness was terminal. The family had woven a tall tale about how it was a non-malignant echinococcus and would soon go away. I was not aware of this story until later. My mother had a lot of practical sense, and it was difficult to fool her. So, as soon as I arrived, she asked me point blank, looking me straight in the eyes:

"Do I have the cursed one? (Εχω το καταραμένο;)," meaning cancer. She had seen how a neighbor, Mr. Pitas, the very one who had offered to support me through high school, had passed away after suffering for months before he succumbed to cancer.

Unwary, fresh from America, always preferring the truth, I told her what I knew. She then, business-like, asked my younger sister to have me buy her some nice underwear because she did not want the neighbors to see her in her regular ones when they would come to prepare her for burial. She asked for the blood-stained sheet she had kept all her life since her wedding night; she wanted to be buried with it. This bloodied sheet was proof of the proper loss of her virginity.

"I've never cheated on your father," she told me proudly, fixing a meaningful glance at me.

She turned on her left side, facing the wall, and spoke no more nor accepted any medication. She died three days later.

Not even a thank you

Although regular correspondence continued, no one wrote to thank me for my "unselfish" act after my father's will was opened; quite to the contrary. My sister and brother had strong disagreements, and lawsuits may have been contemplated. In time, each approached me, requesting that I side with their demands against the other. I declined.

One time, when I was in the States, I received a call from my brother in the middle of the night. He ranted about how I had conspired with our father to deprive him of his inheritance for my own benefit! I could not believe my ears. I tried to tell him he had gotten the lion's share, and I had gotten *nothing*. I simply hung up because there seemed no way to make him see how wrong he was. To this day, I feel I made the right decision to reject my inheritance.

My parents

It is remarkable that even though I refused to accept anything from my father's inheritance, there came a time when another sibling started accusing me of having influenced our father in a way that disadvantaged them. Still, another former family member formally accused me of selling my son's property in Greece and "pocketing the money." Heaven forbid! Some family members still believed this outrageous lie even decades later until it came under direct light.

∞∞∞∞

I am not superstitious. But sometimes, it feels like there is a curse upon family greed. I have had enough experience with relatives and property. The two do not mix well together. I witnessed my ex's mother and uncles tear each other apart for years over an old country house. I have learned about several similar cases centering around how family members tried to exploit each other unfairly, and I have been personally victimized big time in this regard.

Such things have turned me into a cynic regarding family love. I want to congratulate those who claim they have it and live harmoniously with their relatives. I must admit, if you asked me, I do not know of any. Where there is no property, such family strife may be absent. Mostly, however, a realm of hypocrisy prevails. My point of view gets confirmed periodically owing to a lawyer friend who occasionally brings such cases up.

As if justice had a way of correcting things, when my brother found out his turn to die had come, he had his wife offer me the hotel. I declined the offer.

"The hotel is yours," she said. I replied I did not need it and to "be sure to mention that to my nephew Diamantis." I kept a steady course concerning my father's properties. I did not want any part of them whatsoever. Still, I had failed to receive the relatives' expression of gratitude.

Family apology

In the winter of 1997, I covered all expenses for my siblings and their spouses to come to America for a couple of weeks' stay at my Pullman, WA, home. We enjoyed a few happy moments together. My sister Chrisanthi prepared excellent meals. I played Greek songs on my bouzouki and guitar, and we sang and danced. One instance that stands out is related to my father's inheritance.

We were all seated around the dinner table, enjoying a good meal. During the back-and-forth exchange, my sister's husband got angry at my brother for some reason.

"You ought to fall on your knees before your brother and thank him. No one would have done what he did for you," he told my brother. Although I was grateful someone had finally acknowledged a significant gesture, I wished to deter a developing fight. I stepped in saying:

"I haven't invited you all here for that. No need to humiliate Antonis." Antonis was my brother.

∞∞∞∞

The following day, I invited them for a plane ride. They had never been on a private plane before and were very circumspect. Not all could or would participate. To allay their fears, I flew my plane, a Cessna 337, around the airport with my wife as a passenger to allow them to see me take off and return safely. Then they decided it was OK to hop on with me, but not before my brother had crossed himself a couple of times as per the custom when seeking the protection of one's religious avatars.

As I hoped, the magnificence of the Northwest, within a stone's throw of the Canadian border, took my relatives' breath away. Lake Pend Oreille's azure dominating the landscape rivaled Greece's

Meditteranean blue. The endless carpet of evergreens, including pine trees, firs, and spruces, greeted us joyfully as we dove in for the steep descent onto the Sandpoint airport, and our safe landing presented another opportunity for my passengers to cross themselves. I parked the plane and tied it down. We then hopped into a car loaner, the kind many out-of-the-way airports offer for free, and drove to town.

While having lunch at a popular restaurant, the conversation came close to the long-wished-for apology. How does one apologize for having tossed you out in the streets as cruelly as I had been? What if you come from a society that is not too keen on apologizing, on saying sorry?

Words are free. Why were they reluctant to use such a simple salve to soothe my festering wound? What were they afraid of? Does one lose face by admitting error? I thought and hoped the time had come to hear the damn words. Alas, in vain.

∞∞∞∞

The next day, I almost got my wish. My younger sister, out of the blue while making her excellent bread "with love," as she would put it, in my kitchen in the States, said:

"We mistreated you!" I continued playing my bouzouki by the kitchen table, not quite believing my ears, while pondering the long-awaited apology in musical silence. I presumed that was her way of expressing regret for her part in the cruel massacre of my future.

Why hadn't any of my family apologized all these years?

For one, it was not part of the social tradition. My parents, being in a position of family authority, could not possibly feel they had anything to apologize for to us, their dependents. They might not think they did anything wrong, given the social setup and their motives. Or that expressing regret was viewed as losing authority.

My sister's spontaneous apology in my Pullman, Washington, kitchen surprised me and set my thinking in motion. She must have considered the apology for a long time and verbalized it at the first convenient opportunity she found. No one else was in the kitchen then; the others were in the living room. Did my sister choose the occasion precisely because our siblings were not present and because she felt embarrassed to apologize in their presence?

Decades had elapsed since the infamous expulsion from the family hearth. If I kept a count, I would say my father, mother, brother, and older sister still owed me an apology. After all, I visited them in Greece several times and brought presents and some money. I even drove my father to my "hole" in Psarofai, where my wife and I spent dreadful months. I wanted him to see what the family had condemned me to. I must have wanted to hear the damn words "I'm sorry," but never did.

So, my sister's apology took me by surprise, as I had given up waiting for one. And I said nothing. Still, her "We mistreated you" was lame. It was indirect; it lacked contrition gravitas. It could have been "I apologize for my part in hurting you," "I feel sorry we mistreated you," or "I regret my part in hurting you," and the like. Or, it could have been the golden words, as appropriate as can be: "Forgive me for my part in harming you those days." Those words were not uttered that day or any day afterward. That was the verbal gem I, yours truly, was not granted. And I still craved to have been graced with and should have been.

There was a certain complacent insensitivity in all of this. The group mentality was on their side: they were all bound together by common guilt; they must have discussed the event often in my absence and, of course, without my representation. I can imagine how their thinking became entrenched and crystalized over time by mere self-interest. No one wants to feel guilt or live with it, given a choice. I have no idea what discussions occurred or how they explained the "event" to others in the community or extended family. It is entirely possible the war years and the constant struggle for a living may have played their part in fraying the social fabric.

One thing is for sure, fair-minded reader: do not expect fairness in a family dictatorship – they all towed Father's line. He had to be correct (and why not the other members as well?), and I was the renegade, as wrong and deserving of his punishment as can be.

Rationalization is a free commodity.

∞∞∞∞

My older sister never apologized for her part in my expulsion. She was probably guileless and ingenuous in her way.

As for my mother, in all fairness, I feel obligated to consider that bag of groceries she had brought to be delivered to me in Patras at my friend's house as an apology, her way of saying "I'm sorry!" Along the same lines, my parents' later treatment of my little daughter in my absence should also be taken as a form of apology, other factors notwithstanding.

∞∞∞∞

As mentioned earlier, when we were alone in a Patras clinic just two days before her passing, my mother said she had missed me very much over the years. I broke up and fell to my knees by her bedside, crying uncontrollably. Too little, too late. The emotion grips me to this day.

One remarkable incident stands out. About fifteen years after the irrevocable family ostracization, I returned to the United States via a detour through Greece in the early seventies after completing a 10-week study in the Soviet Union, sponsored and financed by IREX (International Research and Exchanges Board). I had contracted what could have been walking pneumonia. My nose was plugged, I had a searing headache, and I ached all over. I felt miserable. My mother noticed my condition and wanted to help. She used to employ her practical medical knowledge with family members and even strangers in the neighborhood or travelers passing through our hotel and restaurant. She prepared herself to administer her cure. But I would not, could not, and did not let her touch me.

Why do you suppose?

∞∞∞

Was I looking for their apology, anyway? I must have been, and it is natural to have been. I was the wronged party, the victim. Validation is an innate need.

And where was my brother's apology?

As I think about it, like most people, I have had relationships with non-family members that are of better quality and much closer. My relationship with my brother, all in all, was closer than with any other family member. Still, it was not of the closest kind. I did not find love as the family glue. Instead, I sensed a common and constant dunning – you owe me because you got an education thanks to me; I put my shoulders to the wheel for your education, etc. – an absurd claim; I need money to remodel the hotel, buy a car, and the like; make me a loan, and I'll repay it – money he'd never return. Ad infinitum.

However, he showed a mellowed side towards the last decade of his life. He asked me to visit more than once and insisted I use his Mercedes in Greece. "He'd like that," his wife told me. He even set me up at the local beach hotel and paid for it on two visits. But I left some cash for that under the folded screen of his computer. And when I finally visited, he put on a real gala with αρνί ψητό (arni psito) -- expensive catered roasted lamb, with traditional music and dance. My sister Chrisanthi and her entire family were also present. We had a great time.

During my last visit, he wanted to show my companion and me a secret drawer he had built under the age-old family dinner table. He bent under the table and pulled a little handle. He brought out some weathered and dog-eared documents. They were embassy translations relating to my scholarly projects to support postponing my military service; they dated back to the sixties, more than fifty years earlier!

It became apparent my brother had been hiding more than some old, dog-eared pages in that secret drawer; he had been nurturing his pride.

"I'm proud to have a brother like you," he said. He would access that drawer whenever the occasion called to flaunt his relationship with me, his wife told me.

There are no words to describe the emotions of moments like that.

When he was later diagnosed with prostate cancer, he was moved by my offer to pay for his operation –it felt like he now had a real brother, he related. After all, I had done so for my father and later for my mother to ease their way out of this world.

It was sometime later when Voula, his wife, called me to repeat an offer:

"The hotel is yours if you want it," she told me.

"I don't want it," I responded. It was the same old response. Later, Voula repeated the offer again after Brother died. I advised her to call my nephew, Diamantis, and inform him that I did not want the hotel.

He now owns it.

Two days before he died, my brother told me on the phone he wanted to see me. He had something to say to me. We never had that conversation. His wife told me after he passed away that he loved me and was also jealous of me. I can understand that.

My poor brother! He was not blessed with my inordinate ambition, although he had a good intellect. As my brother, it was impossible to avoid the endless unfavorable comparisons that were so prone to come his way in the close community in which he existed. The inevitably unfavorable comparisons must have caused an enormous and constant emotional strain. He must have resented me and must have been jealous and conflicted. I believe that is natural.

But he was proud of me, he said. It was a pride arranged by fate for which he had to pay. He was a victim in his own way.

My apologies, brother!

∞∞∞∞

Voula, my brother's wife, stands out as the only person who completely understood the gravity of the family-wide expulsion of me. She was not a party to it, as she and my brother met many years later. From the very start of our relationship, she showed complete empathy and understanding without any prompting on my part. I do not know how she managed to internalize my side! And she went out of her way to make my stays in Greece as pleasant and restful as can be. She more than made up for the lack of contrition on the part of my father's family. I feel I owe her a genuine debt of gratitude.

Rest in peace, Voula!

We need love

Does everyone need the love of their family, of someone? Do we have an intense desire to be loved and nurtured? Psychologists think so. Some will even go further, prescriptively propounding we must offer attention and love to others as a source of happiness and satisfaction.

I knew I needed love. The need for my paternal family's affection was clearly evidenced in subsequent years as I kept returning to visit and acting as if that shocking day of my expulsion from the paternal home had never occurred. Although I had not forgotten, I had forgiven. However, my forgiveness may have had ulterior motives. Holding grudges is not a good idea; it harms us more than anyone else.

Indeed, we need to be loved and to love. At least, I sensed I did. However, on that infamous day when I was banned from Father's house, *my ability to love and to believe words of love were forever cauterized* as if my essential DNA had been altered.

What we had in the family may have been some kind of love based on mutual dependence and a *lack of alternatives.* I clearly thirsted for pure στοργή (affection) but never tasted it. I have concluded over the years that my father's moral hold over me was most likely linked to my need for family affection or affection of some kind. I needed to love my family and to be loved by them. I craved to exist in a family context, ideally rooted in family love.

This is what made me irremediably vulnerable.

∞∞∞∞

The time came when my modest successes in America brought pride to the family, and my financial help was sought. The family member they had ostracized began bringing them intangible benefits; it filled their hungry soul with pride; it raised them in the eyes of the community. They gained respect.

Who does not crave respect?

I personally did not intend for that to happen. I was focusing on my success for my own sake. But benefit them, I did. It was a byproduct of my ambition and hard work. I cannot say I did not like it myself. That they did not deserve it is another story.

They began treating me very well, especially my sister-in-law. They showed me unusual consideration. While I was taking my leave one time, I even heard my father say "I love you" to me. I had never heard him use the words with any family member before.

Did I believe him, do you think? Given the financial realignment, wasn't that too little, too late, or even dubious?

∞∞∞

While living our lives, events take control. A significant amount of wisdom is needed to navigate through life without causing harm to anyone, especially those we care about or should care about. We are not always equipped with the requisite wisdom at the right time to avoid hurting people. We carry in ourselves the potential for good, compassion, kindness, and empathy, as well as evil. We are capable of atrocious acts of unimaginable cruelty. A primary task is to recognize our human nature and keep evil under control.

Maui 1994. My American family

10. Professional dissatisfaction

Career crisis

It was 1976. I was 38 years old. I had been in the States for 16 years, got my B.A. and Ph.D. degrees, and was a full professor with tenure. I had published three books and several scholarly articles. I had started several research projects, all heavily utilizing IBM mainframe computers. My university provided me with a generous budget to carry out my work. I devoted my entire time to research when not busy with my light teaching load. I also established contacts with prominent colleagues throughout major U.S. universities and abroad. Besides being the editor of the University of Idaho Research Foundation Language Series, I also served on the editorial board of the renowned Slavic and East European Journal for a period.

In 1973, as one of 25 U.S. exchange professors, I was granted a fully-funded IREX (International Research and Exchanges Board) grant to the Soviet Union. I established scholarly contact with the Soviet Academy of Sciences, where my book Phonology and Morphology Index (www.koubourlisbooks.com) was warmly received. I also participated in national and international conventions as a paper presenter and/or organizer of scholarly conferences.

My *Concordance to the Poems of Osip Mandelstam (Cornell University Press, 1974),* which took four years to complete, must have impressed a scholarly publishing house enough to ask me to produce another concordance of another poet's works. I was flattered and considered the proposal. However, when I found out there would be no honorarium, I rejected it out of hand. Such scholarly exploitation is not uncommon. The "exploiters" hope the lure of publishing would entice compliant victims like professors eager for recognition by their colleagues and institutions.

There were requests for guest articles and scholarly conference participation. There were even national and international requests for apprenticeships under my direction. I did not have time and was running out of academic steam.

Scholarly swindle

What broke the camel's back was the dishonesty of a colleague from a midwestern university.

I had been working for a couple of years on a collection of articles for another book on a Slavic linguistics topic. As it was a period of publishing austerity, a fellow Slavic scholar and his publisher friend offered to help publish the collection. At a meeting during one of the conferences, I agreed to submit the book material to them and waited for the next step. When the book finally came out, my esteemed colleague's name was on the cover, and my name was mentioned in the introduction. Such an act of dishonesty upset me very much. Scholars are supposed to be honorable people. As is generally known, attribution is in the true scholar's bones, and plagiarism is unacceptable.

I was utterly disgusted. I remember walking around campus for some time, trying to digest what had happened. I shared my grief with the dean. There was little he could say and nothing he could do. I was the victim of a scholarly swindle. I commiserated with some colleagues from other universities and considered the alternatives. I did not want to get embroiled in a scandal, as my publishing zeal was running out of steam. Inertia took over, and the door cracked open for other possibilities.

∞∞∞∞

By this time, I had realized that no matter what I did, there would never be enough money for my family and me to improve our lives. I recall noticing my colleagues leading very modest lives, wearing old clothes, and aggressively counting their pennies. I was struck by the meekness of demeanor and humble appearance. My wallet contained a few dollars year-round. It was an austere form of existence. A professor's salary, even a full professor's salary, was insufficient for my goals. My salary was consumed by life's necessities; bill-paying was always in arrears.

The handwriting was on the wall, and it was depressing. That was not the future I wanted for my family and me. There was no money to pay for my children's longed-for Ivy League education, Hawaii vacations, or travel abroad, which I had been dreaming about. Other people in our midst, members of the upper financial crust, had the means to satisfy all the wants and desires of their chosen ones. Why couldn't I do that, too? Why couldn't I break through the poverty barrier if I was smart enough to get a Ph.D.?

Something else was needed to augment my income.

But what?

I looked around for additional opportunities. I designed a one-step decorative belt creation mechanism but soon gave it up; it would not make me any money fast. I kept looking and looking. Nothing known to me would take me out of professorial poverty. But I kept searching, reading, listening, asking, and thinking.

A seismic shift?

Had the day come to master a new game? Was I prepared to throw away a successful professorial career for more money? What was happening to my values? For decades, I had placed education above all else. I had mastered its frugal game for that prized possession awarded to only about 1.2% of the population – the doctorate. Had the time come to turn my back on my goddess, to betray education?

Lest one confuse educational status with education, a clarification is due. I had gotten my schooling, and it was not only in degrees and professorial status but also in my mind -- I had learned to look at things differently. My value system was modified. I saw no sin in wanting to make money. And neither was I about to give up my doctorate, which is for life. The doctorate could serve more than one purpose. It is not only the necessary qualification for a professorial career. It is something more intangible; it is a badge of supreme achievement. Go tell that to the rich person who dropped out of college but forever covets such a degree, even an honorary one. Find me a sane person who would discount the value of such achievement.

Settled then. The doctorate would not be affected by a career change. And it could be helpful in a different way.

Much of our world is based on prestige. Prestige is a marketable commodity. Thus, having a doctorate was far from a liability. Imagine going to a bank to ask for a loan to help with your investment dream. Your financial statement is the first to be scrutinized, but what about your character? Don't you think having a Ph.D. could be helpful?

I had determined to bust through the poverty barrier. But I was not going to marginalize my education to do that. An emotional battle raged within me.

It is not easy to make a career decision when a successful career is going to be dumped. It had taken a lifetime to create that career. It felt like killing something inside you, which you nurtured for a long time, and undertaking a perilous journey into the unknown. Success could be in doubt.

Even my father put his two cents in shortly before he passed away:

"Don't abandon the university," he told me in his most solemn way.

Isn't this interesting? The man who did all he could to stop me from getting an education became its defender. Had he finally understood the value of education?

∞∞∞∞

People constantly change jobs if what they do is not working out for some reason, like dissatisfaction or lack of fulfillment. My professor's career was successful but was not satisfying in some profound way. And it was not only monetary.

Teaching had lost its gleam for me. My professorial ecosystem was severely damaged by a diminution of passion and a loss of excitement.

I was bored with teaching. I was tired of repeating the same thing to minds of limited receptivity. Occasionally, when a bright student came along, the lecture felt like a conversation between the few. Boredom as a factor must not be underestimated. I recall how painful it became toward the end – it was torture. I could not wait for the class to be over, and there came a time when I couldn't wait for my teaching career to be over. To continue teaching began to feel unfair to the students.

I was ready for a transition.

Ennui can be a killer. Your creativity depends on your state of mind. If one's joie de vivre is conducive to creativity, boredom is not. I wonder if leaving my profession was not like a personal supernova event: I had spread myself out and gotten involved in several projects. I was spent.

I could not see that I was making a difference. I had lost my bearings. My focus on getting the full professorship was the last rung, and what was looming after that was void. And that boded ill. My horizon was in dire need of an extension.

My malaise was contagious. My family began to feel the lack of oomph, the absence of my usual zest for life. It was gloomy being around me. The more the pessimism spread over my ailing psyche, the less my awareness and ability to discern. My quality of life diminished. I became less patient and more irritable. It was not fun being around me.

I needed a radical change, a resetting, and more material means for a better life. A better life without money may be possible for a saint, but not for one who wants to see the world, show it to his family, share a better life with them, and make some difference. I wish I could paint a better picture that money is not essential and that I tightened my belt and took the moral, self-abnegation road as most of my colleagues did.

But it would not be accurate.

∞∞∞∞

I needed time to think about my next big career move. My sabbatical was coming up as if the universe had designed it that way. University faculty at most universities follow a long-established tradition: every seven years, professors are given a year off teaching with full salary privileges while pursuing some favorite research issue. For me, this was a most opportune opportunity. Time off from teaching was just what I needed, precisely what was necessary, providence at work.

Lethal chess?

One of the things I found time for was chess. I liked chess and was reasonably good at it. One day, I played chess with Jon Warren, a friend and the then-legal counsel for the University of Idaho. It was the first of the month. We were in his university office. While our chess-playing was in progress, several young people, one after another, knocked on the door and politely handed Jon an envelope. Of course, I wondered what was going on. Out of politeness, I said nothing after the first envelope was delivered. With the second one, my curiosity and imagination went to the max. *Was Jon on the take?*

The third visitor handed Jon not an envelope but a check. Like a mouse trap, my mind snapped. Jon was definitely on the take, I thought. There was no doubt! Lightning-like, I visualized Jon using his position for illegal but very profitable affairs. My mind harked years back to a Sacramento State College financial official who had used his position to run an escort service exploiting female students in need. My impatience could not be contained:

"Forgive the impertinence, Jon. Do you mind telling me what's going on here?" I articulated as politely and guardedly as possible as if stepping into a minefield. I expected "None of your business" to be a reasonable response.

"It's the first of the month," Jon responded calmly. "I have a few rentals, you know."

No, I did *not* know. In a flash, I was forced to make a nose-dive to reality. Far from a scam, Jon was engaged in a legitimate sideline. I felt a sensation of irrepressible interest seizing control of me. My mind had difficulty focusing on the chess game. What had been an absorbing activity a few minutes earlier was now getting in the way. I was impatiently waiting to find out more about Jon's money tree.

"Checkmate!" exclaimed Jon jubilantly. Jon was my chess student. I had taught him to play chess. This was the first time he beat me. He beamed, unable to contain his joy for beating me, his teacher! However, he understood what my problem was.

"Let's take a ride," Jon suggested after the game. We got into his car for a short ride around the university district.

"You see that white house over there?" Jon asked, pointing at a fifties construction of a free-standing structure. "It's mine!" It was clear Jon was proud of his possession. And who would not be? "Here's another one," he said as we turned into the next street. He showed me his fourteen houses in less than an hour! Each house, one after the other, felt like a massive nail of envy dropping into my greedy soul. Was I ever impressed! This was not a brilliant article or a book published by some coveted scholarly press. This was *wealth*, the kind that puts more than enough food on the table and much more than fanciful intellectual pride in your chest. This could be my hammer to bust through the poverty barrier.

I could now understand why Jon's residence was one of the best in the area -- these rentals had paid for it.

A fire ignited in my scholarly mind. Let's face it: we need money for just about anything in this world. As one goes through life, one hears varying views about money. It does not matter how one regards money. Money is a magnet, attracting everyone, albeit with varying strength. We need money to improve our lives and the lives of our families; money to pay for food, clothing, health, transportation, education, vacations, and more.

Jon noticed my powerful reaction and agreed to explain how he did it. He acquainted me with a small book with interest amounts and rate tables. In this pre-personal computer age, such info was rather esoteric. Bankers and Real Estate people used those tables. Jon gave me an expired edition, and, lest I entertained other ideas, he made it clear I was on my own.

A side job?

Jon's example kept invading my brain. Why couldn't I stick to my professorial niche and have a profit maker on the side? After all, wasn't that what Jon was doing, juggling two jobs? Evidently, his legal occupation did not interfere with his real estate involvement. One job provided stability and status. The other was a remunerative hobby. It is not a bad combination. In fact, I could detect an undeniable inter-dependability.

Why couldn't I do something like that?

Maybe I could, but there was a significant problem.

I did not have the money, and I lacked the know-how. And what about the will?

Real Estate requires considerable sums. As it was, with my professor's salary, I was constantly behind with my bill paying. Every penny had to count.

"You need money to make money," – you hear the popular wisdom repeatedly proclaim. I did not know of anyone who could finance my start. And why would any savvy person take such a risk? I had not proven myself in the business world, and having succeeded in academia was far from a guarantee for commercial success.

As far as obtaining the necessary real estate knowledge, I saw absolutely no problem. Besides, my early life retail exposure and instincts had been proven to me. I felt loaded with confidence, the kind that takes the initiative first and asks questions later. I had faith in myself and in my eventual success. I thought triumph was waiting for me, that a rendez-vous made long ago needed to be kept, and the time was drawing near.

Most everyone wants to be rich; some cannot wait and turn to crime. Opportunities exist for those who prefer working with the system, but more is required. Luck is one ingredient, but you cannot count on it. Believing in yourself and your core abilities might be all you need to get a good start.

As was in my case.

I believed in myself and in my ultimate success. Was I nuts?

Was this the day the scholarly world would lose one of its devoted servants?

Was my game with Jon going to be my last chess game ever? Was I ready to master a different, much more exciting game?

DEMETRIUS KOUBOURLIS PHD

Epilogue

*A*n evening to remember
"In America, income inequality thrives; the economic policies don't favor the poor," my guest blurted out, firing his first shot as we sat down to dinner. "America's Cultural Imperialism is harming local cultures," he continued mercilessly before I could gather my thoughts.

"He's a communist," his wife hurried to toss a label as if diagnosing a disease and to soften the blow. She sat across from me at the dinner table.

"It's OK," I said, putting my hand on the man's wrist – he was sitting on my immediate left. I was trying to compose myself and recover from this unexpected ambush. I had heard such before. It sounded like he was speaking from a prepared script or a script often repeated like a mission. And I steeled myself for more. I am familiar with the type. The man is a retired professor from an Ivy League university. And so is his wife -- two accomplished individuals worthy of every respect.

I tried to conceal my surprise out of common courtesy. I had hoped and was looking forward to a stimulating, recreative evening.

∞∞∞∞

We had met our guests at the famed Boquete Tuesday Market. Boquete is a picturesque village in Panama in the foothills of Volcan Baru. The market is where one meets people from many parts of the world. Often, even on a first-name basis, one can move from vendor's display to vendor's display. A vibrant cultural and language panorama invades the senses: various foods, vegetables, services, and accents offered by Americans, Ukrainians, Germans, Russians, French, Italians, Venezuelans, Jews, Panamanians, you name it. If this seems like a long list, the number of countries clients come from is considerably more extensive. All under one roof. Most of them are expats. They have left their country of origin for various reasons. Some are tourists passing through.

My guests were new arrivals to Boquete, engaged in exploring Panama's retirement potential.

Find that magic intersection

I have learned that politics is not the best dinner topic, as one often slips into groupthink and echo-chambering or a heated argument – the last thing your digestion needs. Although some people consider politics "taboo" during dinner conversations, the potential for a constructive exchange of ideas amongst enlightened, critical-thinking minds may not be discarded. It is wise to contribute a generous portion of empathy and open-mindedness next time you are invited to dinner.

Dogmatic people, *whether from the right or the left*, can be likened to ideological sleepers on the alert for any opportunity to replay their canned message. Underestimating them is an error. They are passionate about their beliefs, and getting their message out is a burning issue. They can be relied upon to be consistent. It is as if they have been programmed this way. They are not interested in your views because they have been to the mountain and got the tablets from their highest authority; they are possessors of the ultimate truth, and anyone else's beliefs do not matter.

My experience with dogmatic people, whether from the right or the left, was not encouraging, although I have known some otherwise reasonable people from both extremes of the political spectrum.

It is almost impossible to change their opinion, as their minds are a priori made up. They have an agenda and are single-minded. Their intellectual approach lacks elasticity and leaves no room for tolerance. And they can be dangerous. These folks can start social upheavals because their views can appeal to gullible minds, and sometimes, their intellectual rigidity gets the better of them.

In my own experience, I've striven to navigate amongst such people with all the skill I can muster. I usually let them spill their message while taking more of their measure and learning something new without making enemies. Political differences can lead to dramatic relationship changes.

I want no part of that.

I believe there's good in everyone and look for it when a promising conversation occurs. When I sense an excellent depth of intellect, I try to convert the conversation into a dialog as I thirst for genuine idea exchanges.

∞∞∞∞

Ideas are powerful entities. They can divide as well as unite people. Their constructive and destructive potential rules the day. I have evolved and have long determined to be *apolitical*. I start from the premise that we all have different ideas but focus on the notion that *our ideas share an intersection*, no matter how different.

This intersection, the "Us" in the picture above, represents what you and I have in common; it can be used as the foundation for constructive dialog. I instinctively look for that. I believe it's the most successful approach to our world of diverse ideas. The more open-minded you and your interlocutor, the more common ground you'll find and the more significant progress you will make in a productive discourse.

I learn much from such an exchange of ideas.

Being apolitical means protecting my intellectual integrity, not surrendering it to the right or the left, and reserving the right to examine issues as objectively as possible without preconceptions.

If it feels uncomfortable to be called by a political label, if such a label does not fit, you're my fellow traveler. This is where I aspire to belong, the enlightened citizenry, the group that prefers evolution over revolution, conversation to confrontation.

The monologue continues

"Globalization and trade policies harm employment and wages," my interlocutor continued unperturbedly as if his mission had not yet been accomplished. He mechanically gobbled his dinner down without paying attention to the exquisitely prepared fare.

"Henry!" his wife interjected imploringly, trying to put the brakes on what must have been a well-known sermon to her. She glanced at me apologetically.

It was in vain; my guest was unstoppable. He was down on America big-time and was expounding from a well-rehearsed list. America was worthless and dangerous, was the message. Communism was the only solution. I fought the urge to interrupt as the man appeared prepared to spew more of his anti-American venom. This was not my first exposure to such a viewpoint, and I am confident it will not be my last.

"There's a lot we can agree on," I finally cut in, relying on my diplomatic best. "Let's face it. We all have different opinions."

"And consider the monopoly of American media, entertainment, consumerism, and the backing of dictatorial regimes," the driven professor pressed on, ignoring my attempt to engage. He was in his zone, visibly delighting at monopolizing the dinner dialog. In a sensible exchange of ideas, I might have eased the discussion to alternatives that had eroded America's pop culture dominance with the advent of the internet before engaging further.

"The military presence, arms race, and ongoing inequality and injustice..." Henry pressed on.

«Что с ним, спятил?» (What's wrong with him? Is he nuts?) whispered my Belarussian companion to me.

"With all due respect, there must be something we can agree on." I managed to squeeze in. "There must be something good about America, don't you think?"

Henry had a point

There was little doubt an exchange of ideas was not in the making. We had been looking forward to enjoying a tete-a-tete with cultured people, colleagues from a famed university. However, once again, in my long life, the distinction between "educated" and "enlightened" was plastered across our table. The man was well-established in his field, with several publications. His academic credentials were not in question, but his lack of objectivity left no doubt. Henry was also forgetting that although entitled to his opinions, sharing them tactfully is not a bad idea.

On the other hand, my guest was partially factual, like it or not. Thanks to unwise leadership, America was guilty of some or all of those accusations and probably more. My mental scan passed over Chile, Vietnam, Grenada, Iraq, …

However, it cannot be true that America has no redeeming value. America has been the most generous member of the international community, providing abundant foreign aid; it has been the most forgiving country in the world.

- Look at the Marshall Plan, the assistance that America poured into Germany and Japan, its main WWII enemies.
- Look at the merciful treatment of its *communist adversaries* after the Cold War. In 1992, the United States spearheaded an effort to aid and prop up the former Soviet Union's 12 new countries that had discarded communism and embraced democracy. Russia was at the top of the list. These were the countries *wrecked* by 70 years of communism, the political system that Henry and his cohorts so ardently advocate. It was America that invited 47 nations to Washington, pleading for assistance of all kinds, including debt forgiveness for these communist countries, its former rivals!

- And didn't America rush to Europe's aid in both world wars?

To fail to see America's *noble* spirit is to ignore its greatness and manifest a deliberate closed-mindedness characteristic of prejudiced, willfully uncritical minds. One can criticize Americans for their errors and shortcomings, for being ethnocentric and ignorant of foreign affairs, but you cannot doubt their noble spirit. They always rise to the occasion. They are usually the first and most generous to assist other nations in need.

Would Russia have been magnanimous had it won the Cold War? Not a chance! Thirty years later, after the fall of communism, there is no sign of gratitude; we are once again enemies as Russia destabilizes Africa and invades Ukraine, vowing to change the world order by marginalizing America, the very country that saved it from communism and its deplorable consequences.

Just think, which country could assume the world lead if not America? Look at human values that matter; do you find more of them in America's enemies, in the alternatives some are proposing? America has indeed earned its lead role but is also a captive of its prize; it cannot retreat without paying an enormous price.

Counterpoint

I saw my immediate task as salvaging the evening in a civilized way. But somehow, I found it hard to proceed without discharging my own broadside:

"Explain just one thing for me, will you, Henry? What's the deal with all those people breaking down America's gates from all over the world, dying to get in but not wanting to go to Russia or Cuba? Why do communist regimes permanently enslave and impoverish their people and build walls to keep them in, but America builds walls to keep them out?"

Henry looked at me as from above, from very high. Then his glance went past me. He wore a smirk of superiority, not deigning to provide an answer.

And I continued, "What if you had spent a significant portion of your days looking for something edible to buy for your dinner, as my lady here, who was born and raised in the Soviet Union, had to do but often returned home empty-handed because the store shelves were empty? Communist countries are poor countries. Their people have been reduced to begging. Communism impoverishes and enslaves people and even robs them of their precious dignity. I've seen that with my own eyes in the Soviet Union and in Cuba."

I had leaped into my turn to deliver my basket of goodies. The fantastic thing was Henry's wife was beaming approvingly. How was she able to live with him, I wondered.

Far from engaging, Henry leaned back in his chair and assumed a better-than-thou, dismissive demeanor, convinced that the importance of his message was so evident as to overshadow any counterarguments or that my points were trivial and did not merit attention. He returned to gobbling up the rest of his meal self-absorbedly. His mission had been accomplished.

∞∞∞∞

Obviously, not unlike Henry, I, too, had my own viewpoint. It would be a mistake to conclude that my views were more "correct" than Henry's. They were simply different. We all have the right to our views. Recognizing this leads to mutual respect and a willingness to listen to each other.

I might have expounded further if Henry were amenable to other people's ideas: America's capitalism, however inegalitarian, is a wealth builder; Henry's cherished communism is not; it leaves a swath of poverty, death, and destruction wherever it may establish a foothold. If capitalism leaves some people in poverty, communism ensures that everyone except for the oligarchy at the top stays poor. Look at the Soviet Union, East Germany, Cuba, and North Korea.

Reality – I would tell Henry -- is outside your conceptual perimeter. Your manifesto beguiles your most utopian instincts; it is an intellectual weapon with apparent appeal but very dangerous in idealistic minds. Belittling America's greatness out of hand makes you a misguided ideologue. In my estimation, there has never been a better country.

America is not perfect, but it's the best country that has ever existed. Indeed, America's potential for goodness remains undiminished – that is the clear and unequivocal message from all those yearning souls putting their lives on the line to get to our border.

True, America's leaders have made and may still be making poor decisions that have cost the country an enormous loss of prestige. However, its fundamental greatness remains unaffected; as the record demonstrates, *America's core ideals align with a better world.*

Henry had missed America's more profound message – the preciousness of freedom -- because he was born and raised in America and had nothing for comparison except his Marxist theories. His stance issued from a realm of great intentions, ignoring communism's disastrous consequences.

I saw no prospect of convincing Henry. I was confident it would be a waste of time. We moved to the living room for dessert, and my partner and I entertained our guests by singing with piano and guitar, highlighting our live-and-let-live approach.

America is my champion

America is infinitely valuable to me. I owe America my remade life, my salvaged education dream. Thanks to America, I rose from the ashes phoenix-like; I dared hope to get reborn. From having no education chances to receiving the highest university degree. From poverty to riches. On its soil, I experienced the taste of freedom and equal opportunity. For me, coming from the darkness and into the light was only possible because of America's values. *America threw a lifeline to me.* It opened its doors to me. "Do you want an education, Demetrius? Here, work for it." Dream and move forward. No arbitrary, man-made obstacles. America's people and institutions facilitated the realization of my dreams; they granted me the chance I needed.

America is my champion.

That is not an exaggeration, a distortion, or a forced opinion. Far from being a show of patriotism, it is an incontrovertible evidence-based conclusion -- just take an objective look at my life's journey in the preceding pages. No other conclusion is possible.

America admitted me to make a better human out of me. It also made an American out of me. Occasionally, non-American contacts ask me why I say "we" when I speak of America. After all, I was born in Greece, the reasoning goes. But they fail to realize that America, the world's veritable melting pot, assimilated me; it made a worthwhile citizen out of me and made us both proud. Being an immigrant in America is not the same as elsewhere. America did not let me in to keep me down. Instead, it placed a panoply of means at my disposal to elevate me to a valuable citizen. In all my years in America, I have never been told the "we" is reserved for native-born Americans.

America is my champion, indeed.

Like all immigrants, I owe America something significant, I am indebted to America for my life's success, and I am expressing my debt here and now. This is pure gratitude; it is basic decency for benefits received, for my American Dream that came true more than once! The American Dream, for me, has not been a success in one endeavor alone, like education, as I have had good results in other ventures, as well. The American Dream is a milieu conducive to success, to whatever legitimate activity your mind focuses on. The system facilitates; it does not obstruct. I carry America with me and within me. *America is an idea of unlimited human potential.* In America, no boundary was placed on my dream's reach or the number of my dreams.

America is my champion, undeniably.

I wanted the best education for my children. They flourished. Our family's success stories include at least two advanced degrees for every member; I am proud of my children's Harvard degrees, Ph.D., and other degrees from major universities. No political clout was necessary. No arbitrary obstacles were in their way. Their ambition and hard work found fertile soil in America. Their academic success would have been impossible in Greece during my time.

What about the immigrants?

If immigrants owe America something, it must also be true that America owes them something in return because immigrants contribute labor, entrepreneurship, industriousness, ingenuity, and cultural diversity. It is not by accident that America is the world's undisputed leader. Immigrants enrich and empower the country in countless ways. It is a thriving, mutually beneficial partnership. Imagine where America would have been without the immigrant multitudes since its existence.

However, some tweaking of this partnership would not hurt. We hear the voices from all over the political spectrum. We see the distortions while a drama continues playing at our border. Can't we do better? We have a crisis-driven policy. If we agree on the merits of immigration, why not focus proactively on systematic, targeted, quality immigration? If untold millions want in, why not harvest the cream of the crop?

We can feel fortunate that some of this is already happening by default, but we can do better!

America, my ailing champion

Although the bloody tears and unhappy face on this book's cover symbolize your current despair, let me note that the torch's smoke is still black -- the final verdict is not out yet.

Never forget divisiveness is the enemy's best ally. The hope is you will not have to break a fever to cure your malaise. You need to keep in mind that in the historical context, your difficult moments are hiccups that pass.

America, loveliest of countries: bring back your serene, confident smile. Entire generations of humans worldwide are grateful to you and recognize, admire, and respect your virtues. Your fundamental virtues shall prevail. If, at times, your leaders lack vision, your core, noble nature will guide and straighten your course again. You have salvaged and shaped countless lives over your entire existence. You have stumbled and risen and will do so again.

I salute you solemnly as I certify my own debt of gratitude.

America, my ailing champion:

You have no equal!

You are in for the long haul.

The world needs you now more than ever!

THE END

THE AUTHOR

The author achieved the highest academic degree after overcoming hunger, homelessness, and hopelessness. He has known failure and success; he has gone from rags and riches and then to rags again, and then... Dr. Koubourlis completed his graduate and post-graduate education in the United States; he was a professor at several major US universities and rapidly rose to tenured full professor. He has spent considerable time in several countries and is fluent in several languages. His exposure to different languages and cultures is reflected in his work.

In addition to his University of Washington dissertation, Dr. Koubourlis produced three books and several articles during his early academic career. With the change in professional orientation, he abandoned academia, devoting his energies to other absorbing activities. While academic publishing was pushed aside, he would never forsake writing; he continued detailed journaling and occasionally sharpened his skills by producing short stories and venturing into writing a novel. However, he never proceeded to publication until now.

Although he has been writing all his life, Sometimes Cruel: Short Stories (2023) and My Ailing Champion: A Memoir (2024) are the author's first non-academic efforts to see the light of publication. More information can be found on Koubourlisbooks.com.

www.ingramcontent.com/pod-product-compliance
Lightning Source LLC
Chambersburg PA
CBHW051138120626
46547CB00012B/848